MOZAMBIQUE
HELL RUN

TRUCKING TALES OF THE WAR

Miguel A. Mitras

Professional typesetting by www.myebook.online

ISBN: 978-0-620-83641-8

Contents

About the Author

Miguel Mitras is a Telecoms Consultant who travels frequently around Africa. He has written a plethora of technical documents in his career, none with any drama.

He lives in Johannesburg, South Africa. Once upon a time he drove big ass trucks.

*For the friends to whom I owe this book,
and aren't here to read it.*

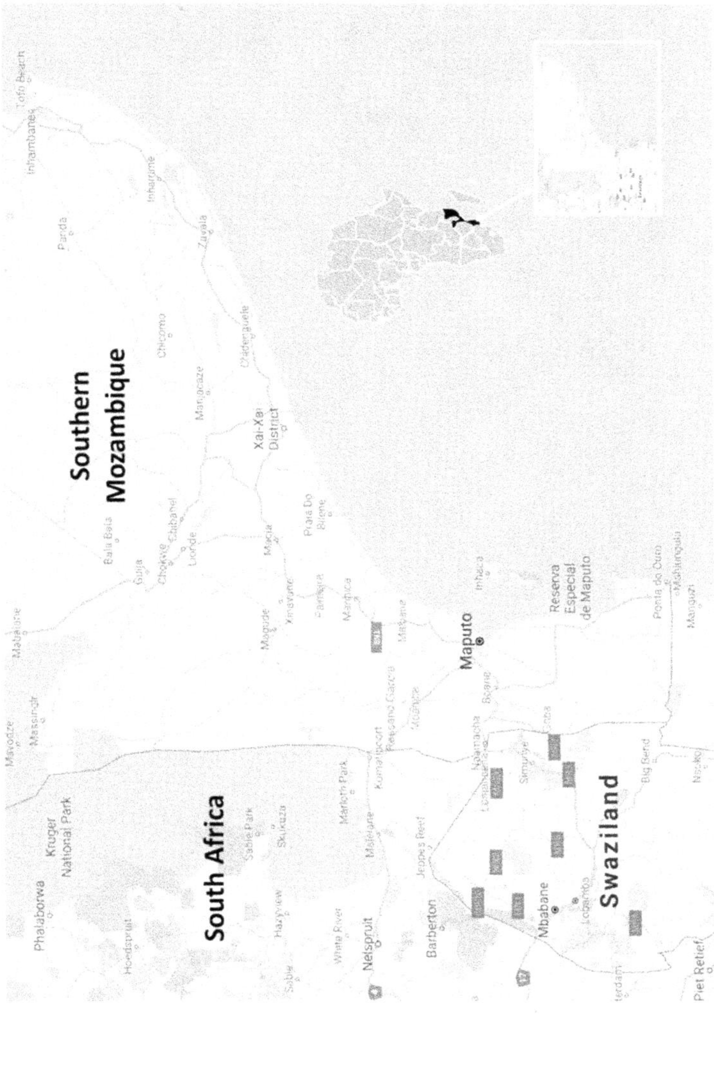
Southern
Mozambique
South Africa
Swaziland
Maputo
Mbabane
Kruger
National Park
Phalaborwa
Nelspruit
Barberton
Xai-Xai
District
Inhambane
Tofo Beach
Reserva
Especial
de Maputo
Big Bend
Piet Retief

List of Abbreviations

DGS Direção-Geral de Segurança (Portuguese State Police until 1969-1974)

DSL Defense Systems Limited

FAM Forças Armadas de Moçambique (Armed Forces of Mozambique)

FAP Força Armada Portuguesa (Portuguese Armed Forces).

Frelimo Frente de Libertação de Moçambique (The Mozambican Liberation Front.)

MML Movimento de Moçambique Livre (Movement of Free Mozambique)

Estado Novo New State or Second Republic (Authoritarian state of Portugal)

MFA Movimento das Forças Armadas (Movement of Armed Forces)

Renamo Resistência Nacional Moçambicana (Mozambican National Resistance)

PIDE Polícia Internacional e de Defesa do Estado (Surveillance and State Defense Police)

SADF South African Defense Force

SNASP Serviço Segurança Nacional Popular (National Service of Popular Security)

ZANU Zimbabwe African National Union

Part I

Truth, the first casualty

1 – Red

A peasant girl with sad eyes stared at the oncoming rig. Approaching the small town of Boane, I dropped through the gears, slowing into a throng of inattentive pedestrians. The previous ninety minutes had been a nerve-jangling run through bandit territory, on a battered road where vehicles were regularly attacked and set ablaze. This intensity eased off as I rolled into the safety of an urban sprawl that extended until it reached the capital Maputo. My rear mirror showed the FAM military barracks fading in the distance, and this girl rooted to the spot like a statue. She wasn't begging; it was as if she only wanted passing traffic to witness her despair.

Beaming, barefoot kids waved as I neared a row of wooden stalls lining the road, just past the railway line that cut through the town. I smiled, waving back at them. Some sarong-clad women looked inquisitively at the truck while the rest stared deadpan. A hundred meters on I slowed to walking pace behind plumes of smoke belching from two small, decrepit trucks. Few vehicles here were roadworthy, pedestrians misjudged speeds, and a horn was sometimes more important than brakes. Some of them had no windows, doors, or even windshields.

An over-zealous, dusty kid tried to outrun me, his

cupped hands lifting higher and higher. I didn't have any candy to give him. It was as if nothing ever happened here; passing foreign trucks must've been the highlight of the day. The engine roared indifferently as I double clutched through the gears.

Passing a row of lethargic tipper trucks outside town, I nearly pushed an oncoming car off the road at the end of the overtaking line. With forty-five tons of flour packed into a forty-foot container, it took a while to gain momentum. Passing two policemen under a row of trees near the Umbuluzi water plant had one hold onto his hat as I brought a gush of wind, while the other wagged a finger at me. Not instructed to stop, the ritual of harassment by policemen who were always hungry—and who always found you guilty of something—would resume next time.

The biggest nuisance in this soaring tropical temperature and stifling humidity, was the heat coming from the engine throwing waves of hot air into the cab. I watched with growing concern as the temperature gauge crept closer to the red. Had the engine overheated on that corridor there would've been more than a broken truck to worry about.

As I gathered speed, a suicidal cyclist wobbled ahead, in and out the road. A gust of air almost took him off his bicycle as I thundered past. More black smoke hung ahead as I down-shifted again for slow traffic, with one eye on the heat gauge which was still flirting with the red zone.

The self-employed, local roadworks keep an eye on foreigners near the checkpoint at Matola. Stepping onto the roadway, armed with a shovel in front of a pothole, an elderly man waited until oncoming vehicles were within sight. As they approached, he busied himself filling it with dusty soil before posing erect, insisting on a donation for the repair. The cab jerked as I crossed, leaving him in a small cloud of dust. I couldn't see how he expected to be paid for his efforts—perhaps this was a startup business operation. Either way, it was inconceivable stopping on this tight road. Besides, it would have taken less than two minutes to fill the hole, yet it seemed to have grown deeper under his supervision.

A man whose stumps swung between his crutches hopped along the sidewalk next to a line of derelict houses. He was another landmine victim. Rumor had it that the government tried to tuck away all the maimed into outlying areas, but it wasn't working. This was Renamo's marketing campaign, a constant reminder of the misery they inflicted on the countryside, and the government's inability to stop it. Mozambique was the world's poorest nation with an equal rating in misfortune. Millions had been displaced, countless had missing limbs, about two hundred thousand children were kidnapped or orphaned, and there were over one million unexploded landmines.

Two young, barefooted black women—one whose upright boobs were showing through a vest—watched the truck approach. As it neared, they shrieked and screamed like delirious youth would do at a pop concert. Pedestrian reactions to foreign trucks rumbling past was often odd, yet always mildly entertaining. But my fixation was only with the engine's temperature; the heat gauge was now just touching red. The sun was really toasting everything today, probably at an oven-ready 44°C.

The customs and police control near Matola Rio approached. Turning into an open space behind the small, square building I spun up the soil. Drying mud from previous rains and other vehicles ploughing the earth had created a sand trap for incoming trucks. Coming to a halt, I waited for someone to collect a copy of the load papers. Policemen stopped cars and talked to motorists across the road; customs officials, along with a handful of soldiers sat under the shade of a tree. A dozy looking woman sat on a blanket selling roasted peanuts, part of another slow-paced day here.

Boom! There was a loud thud, an explosion resembling that of a mortar round. Everything stood still; the bantering and conversations stopped, customs officials and soldiers froze.

Boom! There was a follow up attack.

The tri-axle trailer showed a deflated casing with thin steel cords exposed across the rubber. A tire had exploded from the heat and overload in dramatic fashion; the thread was split from the casing. Its paired wheel suffered the same fate; it was the first time I'd seen two tires burst in succession.

Curious gazes and blank faces followed me while I inspected the damage. They watched my next battle with interest—or out of boredom—between a squeaky twenty-ton hydraulic jack and one of the trailer's axles. The railway sleeper block that housed the jack sunk deeper into the ground as I watched the axle lift by a centimeter only to drop by just as much. I'd have to dig a hole beneath the wheels instead; the jack had lost all its power. Sweat, soil, wheel spanners and power bars; it was a sapping, mid-afternoon rush of blood, and I came out of it looking as though I had wrestled with the soil. And still they stared...

I needed fresh music to unwind; all of my scratched and stretched cassettes had been played out. Anything would do, as the one-tune chorus of the truck's engine hum was monotonous. Within signal range of Maputo, I picked up a radio station. Phil Collins was singing 'Just another day for you and me in paradise'. The disc jockey interrupted the crackling song mid-way, blared something in his native language, and then continued to play it. As the song picked up momentum, and just as the artist hit the high notes in the chorus, the DJ interrupted it again with an on air-caller.

Crr, crr... The sound of static came through the speakers as I lost the station.

The truck was really groaning today. It seemed to be creaking in pain—the chassis, the axles, everything.

I felt my arm burning from the sun coming through the side window as I approached Maputo. Entering Avenida 24 de Julho, a distinct sea smell blew in from the Indian Ocean, followed by a stench from piles of uncollected garbage. Maputo's service delivery was scant. Refuse was collected only every few weeks, and was sometimes burnt inside open metal containers in the street. Parts of the city stunk.

Coming down Avenida 25 de Setembro, I crossed Avenida Albert Luthuli, and came to a stop at the Avenida Guerra Popular—the avenue of the people's war. Waiting for the lights to change to green I realized that I'd overshot the white line by a couple of feet. In Mozambique, traffic lights were parallel to the line where you stopped. There weren't any lights on the opposite side, as was normal at every intersection in South Africa or any country that didn't seek to annoy its drivers.

Mumbling self-disgust at my absent-mindedness I'd have to pull away on a guesstimate. During the wait I looked briefly into the rear-view mirror only to gasp in disbelief. The tarmac was melting with the heat; all twenty-two of my wheels had dug visible double tracks into the road, at least an inch deep. There were no functional weighbridges in Mozambique, and it was compulsory for all foreign trucks to come into downtown Maputo to clear customs. *It's their fault*, I reasoned with myself, trying to relieve the guilt of damaging the road. I knew of no one else loading an accumulated fifty tons on a tri-axle trailer. *A lighter load across a war-torn country wouldn't be worthwhile*, I argued with an imaginary accuser.

Then a thumping, a tingling sensation crept closer. This vibration, music blasting out of a sound system, had invaded downtown Maputo. The noisy car behind me honked his horn impatiently when the traffic lights turned green. He overtook me seconds later as the traffic on my left cleared, throwing a rude hand gesture out his side window. His oversized Ray Bans looked like fakes, complementing a stupid look on his face.

Picking up speed, I approached 'A Casa da Sorte', The House of Luck, a distinct white rounded building that added character to downtown Maputo. Mister Rude Gesture was caught at the traffic light by Avenida Karl Marx, but I caught it on green. Overtaking him while he dawdled, gawking at some passing honeys, I shifted back into the right-hand lane to turn down the next street.

Boom! Another explosion!

A quick glimpse into the rear-view mirror showed shreds of tire blown all over the tarmac. This blistering heat... As his car drove over a strand of loose tire, the thick rubber flapped underneath the chassis, and dislodged the back part of his exhaust. The rude gesture dude spun away from me in a contemptuous snarl. His music was too loud for him to realize that half of his exhaust was missing, and that his car sounded like a hot rod.

I turned right into Avenida Samora Machel, towards the harbor and the customs offices on the Praça 25 de Junho. The Praça was a large tree-lined square surrounded on the one side by office buildings, and it was my final destination until the cargo from South Africa was cleared.

Maputo's road names left little doubt of political doctrines that Frelimo, the ruling party, had adopted. Avenida Vladimir Lenine ran parallel to Avenida Karl Marx, both crossed Avenida Ho Chi Min and Avenida Mao Tsé Tung, which crossed Avenida Kim Il Sung, which crossed Avenida Kenneth Kaunda. Although there was also Avenida Friedrich Engels, to the keen observer José Estaline—or Joseph Stalin—was ostensibly missing from the communist hall of fame. As for popular revolutionary icons, so was Che Guevara. Names admired by the multitudes, heroes of the socialist revolution, but depraved humans, despots and mass murderers to everyone else. With political shifts of recent years, the collapse of the Berlin wall in '89, and Soviet Russia's recent glasnost reforms, these ideological avenues had just about run out of road.

After independence from Portugal in 1975, Samora Machel told delighted crowds that Mozambique would be Africa's first true Marxist country. By its third congress in February 1977, Frelimo had declared itself a Marxist-Leninist vanguard. The country's charismatic first president railed against racism, tribalism, imperialism, and capitalism as he tried to abolish traditional tribal structures and bring in a new communist dawn. Frelimo's program of 'socialization and modernization of the countryside' where a 'modern man' would be created was immensely unpopular. This modern man would live in a society free from polygamy, tribal identity, religion, superstition, and alcohol. Under this initiative, around two million people were relocated, creating a deep resentment within peasant folk—the majority of Mozambique's population.

By 1981, there was little doubt that Mozambique's socialist experiment had failed. State farms, collective *machambas* and *aldeias comunais,* lowered agricultural production, which continued to drop every year. Many peasants had fled the country, or district, rather than being herded into communal villages.

Mozambicans had hoped they'd be better off after independence, but things gradually became worse. A drought in 1983-84, and another one in the present added to the misery. Mozambique was starving. USAID's figures reported that almost two million people would face starvation this year; 1992's estimates were three million. Then there was also that small, niggling problem of a brutal civil war. Compounded with the famine, it would cause over one million deaths by the time the peace treaty was signed.

Marxist fervor gradually cooled. Failed central planning, corruption and totalitarianism had eroded any vestiges of the revolutionary spirit. At Frelimo's fourth congress in 1984, decentralization was stressed, and by 1987, they had privatized twelve hundred state companies. By its fifth congress in 1989, they had dropped the Marxist-Leninist label, although still referring to the revolutionary struggle, economic restructuring was the main emphasis. Conforming to International Monetary Fund and World Bank guidelines, the party began adopting free market principles. Import-export policies became looser and more trucks rolled across its borders. Government censorship was not as tight as it had been, and regulations were less restrictive. It had been quite a political about-face in recent years.

Two light blue Mack and Oshkosh semi-trucks with their flat deck trailers were parked in front of the customs office on a small side road. These drivers had been caught trying to smuggle AK-47 automatic rifles in their diesel tanks into South Africa. There were rumors that these weapons were going to the 'third force', a group behind the political violence escalating between the African National Congress (ANC) and Inkatha Freedom Party (IFP) in the KwaZulu-Natal province.

But guns were foreign currency and could have gone anywhere. Post-war statistics revealed that Frelimo had distributed approximately one and a half million rifles to civilian militia. Others estimate that millions of small arms were in circulation when the government's army was only 30,000 strong. Most buildings and residences of any significance in Maputo had armed guards with Kalashnikov assault rifles.

The AK-47 had become ubiquitous in every sense of the word. South Africans grew accustomed to car-jackings, bank robberies, and cash-in-transit heists committed with these weapons in the 1990s and beyond. Most, if not all, of them had crawled out of Mozambique's black market, sometimes bought for no more than a few dollars.

The two impounded trucks belonged to Braamson transport, the biggest South African operator coming into Mozambique in 1991. Its owner, Braam, had lost another five trucks on the transport run from South Africa to Maputo, all of them set on fire after being attacked.

Transport corridors in Mozambique were collectively referred to as 'the hell run' by truckers and the South African media. The term's origin was unknown to us, but it had stuck, and was apt for a number of reasons. Armed banditry attacking vehicles on all national roads, and the government's inability to protect them with underfed, undisciplined, and inadequately trained soldiers was the center of all angst. Roads that were in terrible conditions, corrupt army officials' black marketeering weapons, drugs, and looted goods only added to the problem. The death toll kept growing with no signs of abating.

My truck's temperature gradually cooled; the gauge had moved slowly and stubbornly off the red. Fixing the truck inside Mozambique was difficult with little access to parts, tools, or repair facilities. Breaking down here was never an option. My rig, a Swedish-built Volvo F12 cab over had a clogged radiator that needed to be looked at; I'd have to nurse it back to South Africa.

Weariness came over me as the day's intensity wore off. Lying back on the seat, head planted on the headrest, I tried to gather my thoughts. Enjoying my first moment of serenity, a vehicle without a muffler interrupted the silence. A line of sparks, like an angle grinder, flew past the truck. A badly dented and faded Ford F100 pickup came barreling towards the harbor. Overloaded with people, the exhaust pipe scraped the tarmac while thick, black exhaust fumes enveloped it. I chuckled. Leaving an oily smell, it also awakened all the surrounding odors, of urine on the sidewalk, the fishy, salty smell from the nearby dock, and a nauseating stench from water puddles.

I needed a payphone to update my boss, Artur, after every trip, so I walked towards Avenida 25 de Setembro, past the famous Continental Café. Two beggars with missing legs were sprawled on the sidewalk, their voices drowned out by the sounds of the busy café. The smell of espresso engulfed the air and waiters shifted between tables as I trudged past. I hopped across the road to the *correios*, the central post office. It had antiquated public phones that still took coins—coins that were worth nothing.

Anyone could make an International call to South Africa for about three minutes at a time even though they couldn't buy a morsel of bread here. The value of the local currency, the Metical, had depreciated by thousands of percent in recent years. There was no shortage of money here, only a shortage of things to buy. They would repair the pay phones, but Mozambique would take much longer to fix. The political contradictions would probably remain, like capitalist trucks rolling down Karl Marx Avenue.

2 – Bewitched

Maputo did not feel like a besieged city. While war menaced around its edges, the capital seemed insulated from the tortured countryside. Everyone appeared content, giving little thought to the political stalemate, or the country's infrastructure being choked by Renamo.

There were occasional blackouts in parts of the city, a signature of sabotage, but this may have also been because of an aging electrical infrastructure. I'd been told that the Renamo rebels blew up pylons on a 270-kV power line from South Africa; then laid mines on routes to the pylons to prevent repairs. Yet, I'd also heard that it was in in fact government forces that laid minefields to keep them out.

'*Cidade do feitiço*' some called it, a city of enchantment. *Feitiço* also means 'a spell'; if you ventured into the capital and stayed a while, you'd understand. Maputo had a Havana feel to it; both cities had a fading splendor and similar African-Latin atmosphere. Occasionally, a gentle breeze would blow in from the Indian Ocean bringing relief from the heat and humidity.

Mozambique has a warm water current running south along its coast which raises temperatures, rainfall, and humidity in the coastal areas. People here were also warm; Mozambicans were mostly a gentle people, which made the fratricide and conflict harder to comprehend.

War had ruined Mozambique, but an economic recovery loomed. Few transport operators understood the political complexities that fueled the conflict. They were brought here by attractive cross-border rates and wages. But they all quickly realized that driving into Mozambique was hazardous to their health.

The corridor from Swaziland and South Africa was called the corridor of death, but it wasn't as if there was a warning sign on the way in. New drivers saw cars and trucks aflame with bodies burning inside; sometimes it was their colleagues. Many only ever did a single trip before quitting, yet others kept coming back. Maputo being the '*cidade do feitiço*' may have had something to do with that.

I'd recently befriended a very personable *mestiço*, Cuca. My boss had contracted him as an independent agent to help clear our loads quicker. Getting past the bureaucracy in Mozambique's customs process could challenge one's sanity; standing trucks were lost revenue, which didn't seem to bother the civil servants at Mozambique's *alfandega*.

I met Cuca at the customs offices during a quarrel I was having with them. It was more like threatening to offload forty-one tons of Coca-Cola and Fanta cans on the pavement, on a public street, unless they got their s★★t together. Fairly new to this gig, I'd been stuck in Maputo for over a week and a half, and was out of clean clothes and money. Cuca overheard my tirade and offered to help. Well-connected and adept at the bureaucratic vernacular, he became a big trucking operator himself in years to come. Whenever I arrived from South Africa, he invited me out, or offered his home for the night.

One evening, we were having supper. The Clube Mini-Golf, a seaside restaurant with a miniature golf course had survived almost unchanged from the colonial days. Probably Maputo's most popular nightclub in 1991, it had a Brazilian ting to it with its coconut culture. Rhythmic music and dancing that was sensual and flagrantly provocative would beat until the early hours, just as hot and spicy as the prawns they served.

We arrived early enough to get a table and enjoy a restaurant atmosphere. There was light jazz oozing in the background until 22h00 when the establishment switched to a nightclub. We settled into the sounds of knives and forks clinking plates, and people gesturing to one another animatedly. A weight of exhaustion came over me as soon as we sat down. I stared at my hands resting on a clean, white tablecloth. They seemed to be permanently dirty, full of calluses from pulling ropes, tying down loads, and changing tires. To see how clean they were, I rubbed them against the linen and saw no marks or streaks. Gosh, my mind was tired.

Looking towards the doorway, I saw an elderly European man walking out with an attractive black teenager. Investment consortiums and aid agencies had brought an influx of foreign workers into Mozambique. Expatriates, notably Nordics and Scandinavians drooling over local girls were a common sight. The Portuguese had left a legacy of exquisite *mestiço* women who strutted around while I pretended not to notice. But everything here was super expensive, restricting the clientele to the wealthy, the pretenders and the hustlers.

Being European, in my mid-twenties, long haired—in typical 80s mullet style—and driving trucks was a rare sight in Mozambique. My host was keen to understand trucking; was it easy to learn? The exchange, in Portuguese, went like this;

"Sure," I replied, "but you need to have a feel for the machine. If you don't have the skill to take a heavy load down a mountain pass, it'll pull you down with it."

He interrupted, "Is it because the truck can't brake in time?"

"You shouldn't ride brakes down a mountain pass, because they'll overheat. Keep them cold for when you need them. And find a gear that holds the truck steady on the downslope, along with the Jakes."

"Jakes?" he looked puzzled.

"Yah, it's an engine brake, the Jacob's brake, the one that sounds like a machine gun?"

"Ah, yes," he replied. "They want to ban trucks coming into the *baixa*, to stop them making a racket."

I chuckled at the thought. Truckers had many uses for the 'Jakes' engine brake, including frightening pedestrians off the road. Although intended to slow down, or retard, the engine revs; for egos it was more about imposing your presence. But it was never a good idea to use it on the transport corridors—something I realized later. The reverberating thunder-like sound would alert bandits that a truck was near. They'd created the Jakes to assist in steep downhills, not to sound cool. But boys will be boys.

"We have a saying that the truck is the boss, not you." I carried on philosophically, not sure what I'd say next. "Then there are the different gearboxes you have to master. Then there's driving sense." I carried on with a term I made up in the moment. "Let me explain. You are caught behind someone on a winding road, on a downhill, you know, a mountain pass. There's a truck in front of you. It's a dark night and you are following those red taillights. After a while, they begin to hypnotize you. You can't overtake because it's too dangerous, so now you're stuck behind him. After a while, you become fixated with those lights. If that truck in front goes off the side of the mountain, you will follow it."

I paused as he shifted into a ponderous silence.

"Yah, trucking's a rough life. It's dirty, sometimes frustrating. We have to tie down loads when we don't run containers. Two tarpaulins, nets, and many ropes. The three-hour workout to sail up a truck, 'twill keep you entertained," I added, trying to keep the conversation going. But suddenly, my eyes were locked onto this beautiful young woman sitting a few tables away.

She was gorgeous with strikingly long, dark hair. There was definitely a tinge of mixed race, as noticeable as her full lips. Modestly dressed and sitting fairly distant from her boyfriend, there was only a calm, sweet air of innocence around her. It was as if she wasn't a part of this sultry atmosphere. For a split second, we looked at each other, but her hazel eyes quickly disappeared behind the brown menu. Seconds later she put it down and smiled at her companion. I was suddenly aware that I'd been staring when my friend's chattering clicked me out of the hypnotic lure. He asked something about what I'd said, or about what he was saying. I hadn't been paying attention.

"Yah, hum," I stammered. "You know, there's also a sixth sense about the road."

"What's that?"

"*Sexto sentido.* You're driving on a dark night, and everything is calm. It's just you and the road." I continued, trying to sound dramatic. "You've got some good blues playing, you're on rhythm, the engine's humming along. Now something tells you to slow down. Your mind says no, but for some inexplicable reason you take your foot off the gas. In the next moment, you're nearly on top of a slow-moving truck; it's crawling along with no working taillights and no reflectors. If you hadn't slowed down in time, there could've been a nasty collision."

I couldn't shake the image of her eyes peering over a brown menu, just hanging there.

"Hum, yah, a coke, Coca-Cola and a salad and…" I pointed to one of the prawn options on the menu, caught unaware by the sudden invasion of the waiter. He nodded, took my friend's order, folded the menu and slipped away, leaving me wondering if he remembered everything we asked for. The night settled into men's banter and talk about the road, a euphemism for the corridors. Before I knew it, the ambience had changed, music started blaring and young girls were swinging hips on the dance floor. I was too worn-out to stick around, or pay any attention. '*Vamos*? Let's go?

"Cigarette?" A cheerful face asked, puffing an imaginary cigarette. We weaved past bodies at the main entrance and made our way down the stairs. People were trickling in and out of the building, a car spun away from the club, and another one, overloaded with people, arrived. Luxury cars, not-so luxury cars—they were all here as the club began to come alive.

The new trend was seeing cars and motorbikes stolen in South Africa re-registered here via the usual, all too common corruption. Many couldn't afford cigarettes, let alone the entrance fee, much less expensive sedans. A young man muttered incoherent sentences as they escorted him onto the grass so he could throw up. Some couldn't afford the expensive drinks, so they topped up at a cheaper joint on the way here, or so it seemed.

"*Queremos boleia*!" We want a ride! Two young black women obstructed the path towards our car. Looking coarse and easy, one was wearing too much red lipstick, which glowed under the dim street light.

"*Vai embora*!" Get lost. I waved them away.

"*Vamos para a baixa*." We are going to town, they solicited further.

"*Boa viagem*." Bon voyage. I said sarcastically. They giggled amongst themselves.

"*Ya, vamos*!" Yes, let's go. They persisted, so did their smiling.

"*Vocês são meninas*!" You are little girls! I scolded them.

"*Não é assim*!" It's not like that! One protested, wagging a finger in denial. My friend shooed them away. Maybe it wasn't like that.

Driving down the Avenida Marginal towards town, we saw private boats rocking gently at the Clube Naval, the old, Portuguese yacht club. Pairs of policemen walked along the esplanade under rows of palm trees. It was a pleasant drive, watching the corniche slope gently towards a ridge that overlooked the sea. My thoughts drifted in the calm.

But the city appeared quickly, a concrete slum of tall buildings with faded walls. Laundry still hung on some balconies at this time of night—the only colorful decorations on this grey land under the moonlight. Colonial architectural influence was still evident, now marred by civil neglect and fading revolutionary slogans on the sides of buildings and walls. It looked like a light blitz had hit the place, something that could unnerve anyone who had seen it before the insurrection of the 1970s.

Lourenço Marques, as we had called it, was once a beautiful, fashionable city, a colonial paradise for many.

People that once lived or visited here, spoke of it wistfully, or with grand memories. Some buildings still had marble or expensive wooden flooring, a reminder of how nice it had been. You could still see evidence of the theatres, cafes, and charming side streets that once bustled with tourists. Now decay and dilapidation was everywhere; in the preceding years it was common to find sewerage systems blocked and squatters living on roofs of buildings. Toilets had become rooms and apartments were overcrowded as villagers moved in with livestock. Where there'd once been elevators, was now just a hole in the wall. Mozambique was a country of beautiful buildings lying in ruins.

Few of the elevators in the high-rise buildings worked, and stairways were always dark because there were no lightbulbs available. Tenants had to trudge up and down the stairs with containers because water did not flow to all the faucets. Many sustained serious injuries from slipping on wet floors from spilling buckets. No one had money to pay for service rates and the municipality could not maintain the city. Maputo would have been even more dysfunctional were it not for a volunteer program—albeit obligatory—for hospital and municipal work.

Museums, markets, and historical places were damaged with little hope of repair or restoration. Yet, despite the rot, Maputo remained an attractive city of many boulevards with acacia, jacaranda, and flame trees. It still had an eye-catching skyline; it still had charm.

We arrived at the customs square where my truck was parked. Cuca again offered his place for the night, mentioning spare rooms and air conditioning. I thanked him and declined. After a couple of squirts of mozzie spray, I drew the truck's curtains and fell asleep within seconds of dropping on the bed.

It may have been ten minutes, an hour, or even three hours—it was hard to tell how long I'd been asleep. A continuous banging on the door penetrated my deep slumber. Rubbing my eyes, I tried to wake before peering through a gap in the curtains. There was no one outside.

Tap, tap, tap! More knocking on the door. I sluggishly wound down the window and was greeted by a pair of 'them' smiling at me. And that awful smelling perfume... They wanted to talk to me. In my stupor, my reply may have sounded obscene. I slumped again on the bed, falling asleep to the whispering amongst two African ladies in the street.

It may have been an hour or more before I was rudely woken up again. This time the tapping on the door was less desperate, but more precise. I shook my head in frustration. Rolling down the window again, I was faced with what I abhorred most; two policemen stood outside the truck. Snappily, I asked them what they wanted; it was to search the truck for prostitutes. They were told to get lost before I lay down again. Policemen jabbering amongst themselves, and my mumbling about my friend's offer of accommodation were dying sounds before I closed my eyes.

A morning sun beat down. With closed windows, the cab became unbearably hot, but conversations outside woke me up first. Vendors were all over the square and activity was picking up. That girl I'd locked onto with was my first thought of the day and I could not remove the image of her brown eyes peering over the menu.

Then I came back to reality.

Bang! Bang! There was a commotion from a row of parked trucks across the street. Two policemen stood outside one of them, banging with a flat hand against the door. Comical Afrikaans cursing came from inside the Oshkosh truck. Behind the officers was a young, fairly attractive black woman with her arms folded, looking very displeased.

"*Jou ma se* …!" Your mother's …! Some defiant profanity came from inside; urban street-slang only a South African would understand.

"Fokof!" The foul-mouthed tirade continued. A moment of silence was followed by the sound of an AK-47 rifle cocking, then an instant hush. The driver's door cracked open with two eyes peeping through the gap. "Fok."

In the next scene of this bizarre event, a colored—our term for a mixed race—South African-driver, still in his underwear was arguing with them on the street. No one batted an eyelid, as if this was the daily menu. He'd been with her the night before; too drunk to fornicate, he passed out after a six-pack or two of beers. They'd come to frog-march him to the *esquadra*, the police station, so that he could settle his outstanding bill. At least that's what I was told.

I asked a friend's wife, a local of Mozambique, about these idiosyncrasies. She chuckled, 'The police are on commission, you didn't know?' With some of these ladies, there were two different rates; one rate for using a contraceptive and another without a contraceptive.

"Ok, so?" I asked, to which she replied, "Using a contraceptive costs more."

Now I was puzzled, but she explained, still sniggering, that using a contraceptive costs more because the ladies say it hurts more.

Most of them, including their clientele, would not be alive in the coming years. There was no cure for the HIV virus in 1991. Understanding of the subject ranged from the superstitious, sometimes just doltish, to the outright spiteful. A street worker interviewed on Mozambican television was asked if she would stop if she discovered she was HIV positive. Her reply was a succinct '*Eu não vou morrer sozinha.*' I will not die alone.

3 – Corridor

All traffic from South Africa towards Maputo was rerouted through Swaziland, a small kingdom country landlocked between the two. The direct—and shorter—route through the Ressano Garcia border was unused by heavy vehicles. In 1983, possibly the first transporter from South Africa to Mozambique post-independence used the Ressano to Maputo route, taking the dirt road from Moamba to Boane. After this semi-truck from Norman's transport, carrying a load of glass bottles was ambushed and torched trucks never used this road again. In 1989, the rebels attacked Ressano Garcia and killed eighty people. To avoid further deaths, a freight train with hundreds of civilians clinging to its sides reversed back into South Africa during Renamo's clash with FAM.

The route we used, passing through the border town of Namaacha towards the capital, was frequently attacked. Although this stretch was perhaps easier to defend militarily than the other one, it was no less dangerous. Traveling on any of the transport corridors in Mozambique was flirting with death, but it wasn't just the roads; in early 1990 rebels ambushed a train bringing Mozambican miners from South Africa, again near Ressano Garcia. Forty-seven people were killed when Renamo detonated a remote-controlled mine that derailed the train before opening fire on the carriages.

Going north of the capital towards Beira, Mozambique's second major city was the most harrowing route of all. It was a twelve-hundred-kilometer drive through the shadow of death. Transiting through the northern province of Tete was a route known as the 'gun run', but also called the 'hell run'. This road linked Zimbabwe and South Africa to landlocked Malawi. Some considered this two hundred and eighty kilometer stretch the most dangerous due to the extent of potholes and number of landmines buried across its path. The road between Beira and Zimbabwe had deteriorated to where it became almost unusable during the war.

This corridor ran through a Renamo 'liberated area'. Zimbabwe soldiers assisted Mozambique's government here—landlocked Zimbabwe needed access to the port in Beira and the oil pipeline between the two countries needed protection. The ambushes on the corridors were as unpredictable as they were periodic, and every road, or railway headed towards Maputo came under constant attack.

There was turmoil and *confusão*—confusion—at the Namaacha border post this morning. Trucks were queuing up but weren't leaving. A story was doing the rounds about a minibus taxi being shot up en route to Maputo and no one was in a hurry to hit the road. Some drivers resignedly went back to their trucks to wait for some order to return while some congregated in groups to discuss the situation. Others ambled back inside the building to find out more from the officials. I joined my friend Joe who was talking with an animated group of travelers. The death toll was increasing as the conversation wore on; it wouldn't be long before the attack expanded to two vehicles.

At the time, I hadn't bonded or interacted much with any of the regular South African truckers coming into

Mozambique—except for Joe, a veteran of Africa trucking, whom I'd known for a few years. He'd been on the South Africa to Zambia and Congo runs, which I'd heard were also grueling routes, in the 1980s.

The easiest way to describe him was a middle-aged hippy with a truck license; a likable, pleasant person with a long beard that fitted his philosophical tendencies. He came from a very strong Afrikaans background, conspicuous in the surname of Odendaal. Aside from trucking, he didn't fit into our normal society; being married to a black woman was scoffed at in apartheid South Africa. Joe could speak four native languages, but in addition to the language fluency, he could mimic expressions, tone, and mannerisms just like black folk. Another friend I'd soon meet through him, named H, called Joe the salt of the earth.

An older, bearded man who came across as someone who'd misplaced his anxiety meds approached our group.

"Please, please, I see you are regulars here. I have very, very urgent business to attend to in Maputo. It's a matter of life and death. I must be there today. Can you please advise me, what must I do?" He went on. Some chuckled and stepped away while Joe stroked his dusty beard and nodded.

One driver remained with us, listening to the urgency in the man's voice with some interest. He scratched his head and then exclaimed, "My friend, buy yourself a bottle of cheap red wine—it's available anywhere here. Stop the car on that first army control just outside of town and down the whole bottle. Then pray. Then just go."

The bearded man gave him an incredulous look, turned around and walked off. He must have thought he was being mocked, which he wasn't. Little did I know that it was the purest, sincerest advice any trucker would give you. They did similar stuff here—red wine was just an appetizer.

My Volvo F12 was one of the faster trucks on the run. She didn't have a noisy Jakes engine brake; this make came with an air brake which was less effective, but she had comfort and speed. Vehicles dallying in front were a hindrance, catching up on the first stretch of road meant tapping brakes all the way behind them. The roads here were ruined through years of neglect and erosion, further swallowed up by the countryside, which made overtaking very difficult. Even though trucks liked to run convoy because they felt safer in groups, I was never comfortable with the idea, because it meant more targets. Besides, I also had business to attend to in Maputo. It was the best time to jump the queue. Looking towards Joe I said, 'I'm gone'.

"The road's hot, maybe you should wait," he replied, watching me heading off towards the offices.

"Mister Miguel, you cannot proceed to Maputo." Those were the words I heard from beneath the spectacles of a customs official scanning my documents. Although I spoke Portuguese fluently, I sometimes pretended not to. When probed about inconsistencies on export forms, it was easier to switch to English.

"Why is that?" I replied, perspiring in the humidity of the darkened offices. Coming from the bright sunlight into this dim space had tightened my eyes; I was struggling to make out the black man's face as I spoke to him.

"The road is very agitated." He went on, handing me back the forms.

"The agents of the load will also be agitated if I don't offload in Maputo today. It was pre-arranged with customs."

"What is in your container?" He asked while dithering around some paperwork on his desk.

"Steel beams and paint, construction." I said, trying to ignore the perspiration and odors of unwashed bodies all around me as I wiped the sweat dripping from my face.

"It is not a perishable load?"

"No, it's worse. Do you see the bumper on my trailer? It was black this morning, now it's white and grey. The paint is exploding inside the container, and I suspect if it stands much longer in this heat, it will paint lines across the road."

"I do not understand your hurry to Maputo with this confusion."

"If the road has been hit, surely the, hum, bandits have gone by now."

He gave me a long stare, stamped all the forms, and handed them to another clerk for further processing. I wasn't sure what to think; he was a little quick in letting me go.

A few kilometers outside Namaacha, the military check-point under a row of eucalyptus trees beckoned me to stop. Two soldiers in green uniform waved the truck down. First, it was a long stare, then the customary five seconds of silence followed by the routine, meaningless question.

"*Você vai para Maputo*?" Are you going to Maputo? One soldier asked eagerly.

"Yah." I replied, forcing a smile, as if there was anywhere else to go to from here.

"*A estrada nao está bom.*" The road is not well. The soldier jumped onto the steps of the cab, held onto the rear-view mirror frame and looked inside. There was never anything to inspect, only what we could donate to them. He eyed a soft drink on the passenger seat, which I handed to him with some cigarettes.

"*Vai!*" Go! The soldier motioned as the other lifted the metal boom.

Pulling away, I looked in the rear-view mirror and saw what must have been the officer in charge walking briskly from behind some trees. Gesticulating, he was having an excitable discourse with the other two. Turning into a long, curving downhill, I saw the soldier handing his superior the soft drink just as they disappeared from sight. I began to wonder if they were at liberty to allow vehicles through the checkpoint, and if the officer was upbraiding them for having done so. Nah, it was just my mind playing tricks on me.

Two sarong-clad women with firewood on their heads walked away from the road. Unless they were foreigners, females weren't allowed to wear trousers. Instead, a cloth fabric called a *capulana* wrapped around the body was the government-approved attire. They were dropping off bundles at predetermined spots on the side of the road which would be collected before sunset by vehicle.

Electricity was a rare commodity here, local water had to be boiled before consumption, and firewood was the main means of energy. Most houses were derelict, or just ruined through years of neglect. Wood burning fires inside them left huge black marks around the windows. Many a wooden window frame, floorboards, and doors had been used for fuel by now. Driving past some houses gave one an impression of a teenage bruised, black-eyed look. Like Mozambique.

The scenic town of Namaacha lies perched on the Lebombo Mountain range. Just past the town, a few twists and turns on the mountain pass came at you quickly, but they were only the beginning of things that could come at you. This was the most torturous part of the journey; some stretches of road was wide enough for one truck and perhaps three quarters of another, but not quite two. That was my estimate. Huge portions of tarmac had been washed away by heavy rains, and elephant grass was growing high on the sides, hiding the true slant of the ground. If you went off the tarmac, you didn't know whether you'd hit sand, flip, or drift towards a plunge down a mountain. Two semi-trucks had recently plummeted into these deep ravines; one of them was a light blue Mack truck with thirty tons of cement on a flat deck trailer. The other was possibly an Oshkosh truck, the white tractor was too badly damaged to be identified from up here.

When facing a truck from the opposite direction, two things were necessary; first you had to tuck in the rear-view mirror. I'd smashed two mirrors into other trucks as we passed inches apart. Secondly, you had to steer with precision, there was little margin for error. Trucks did not slow down on these slopes unless they absolutely had to. When meeting oncoming traffic on this stretch, you faced vehicles at high speeds, misjudging the driving line could be disastrous. Fully loaded semi or articulated trucks, had no braking power on these slopes and the insane tonnage I brought into Mozambique further reduced my braking capability to nearly zero. I'd never get used to pushing hard on the brake pedal while rushing downhill and having that hollow feeling that nothing is happening. While the smell of overheated brakes would persist, the truck would continue to speed up. There's only so much friction brakes can handle before overheating and setting the tires on fire. That's the time you steer and hope for the best; until the road flattened out again, there'd be no brakes.

Then again, even if the truck leaned over to its maximum off the tarmac to avoid a collision, there were still the dreaded '*skorokoros*'. This was an Afrikaans slang word truckers used to describe some Mozambican trucks. They were old and rotting, sometimes their trailers' axles were so misaligned that the tractor in front would miss you comfortably, but the trailer and its container would come right at you. That was the cause of one of my smashed mirrors. Yes, you could choose to go slowly and use a low gear that would hold the rig on the downslopes, but it was never a good idea to give bandits a slower target. You needed speed to carry you into the small climbs, not crawl through them. That's where bandits waited.

As a hill levelled off, a group of green-uniformed FAM government soldiers appeared, walking on the side of the road. One with a heavy caliber ammo belt adorned over his chest, another with a rocket-propelled grenade launcher slung over his shoulders. Shiny copper jacketed death strapped over the uniform looked menacing. From here, everything did.

Another soldier, carrying an RPD, a soviet light machine gun, stared as his comrade waved me down without much urgency. FAM signaled all trucks to slow down, especially foreign ones. All they wanted was cigarettes, bread, or banter to hustle something. Stopping along these turns, or anywhere else for that matter, would've been crazy. Another kilometer down the drag more soldiers emerged, doing the same as I sped up past them. From here onwards you might see more soldiers until Boane or you may not; every trip was different, it seemed.

Rapid thoughts came at me. Up to now I'd been caught up in the hype of bypassing the queue, not giving much consideration to why everyone else was hesitant. I hadn't really thought this through, had I? The idea that the road could still be hot was starting to linger. A good song was playing on the stereo, yet I had this sudden need to concentrate. I didn't want background music occupying any part of my concentration.

Switching off the music so suddenly made me feel alone.

A breeze blowing over the long, dry grass distracted me as I watched it curving gently, enjoying a second of tranquility. Peering back towards the road my hands tightened their grip over the steering wheel. I was staring smack into the projectile of a rocket-propelled grenade pointed at me. I too have fired an RPG-7 in weapons training during national service in the South African Defense Force. The loading is simple; you click off the safety catch and pull the trigger, its destruction at your fingertips. The distinctive sound of a projectile blasting from the hand-held device is a 'swoosh' sound I cannot forget. Then there's the slight tail whip of the rocket as it leaves the chamber before correcting itself in the path of doom. Behind the launcher, anything within a thirty-degree, twenty-meter radius will be grilled from the exhaust. It was that 'swoosh' that echoed in my head, becoming louder the longer I fixated on it.

A heart skipping moment went by before I realized that the soldier wasn't aiming the grenade launcher at the truck. He merely had it parked over his shoulder, like they all did. If that RPG had gone off, the *camarada* behind him would have been roasted. These weapons, on first impression, looked useless against barefooted insurgency, deadly against trucks.

Were they anti-armor, or anti-personnel? It's possible that fragmentation projectiles could be used in small scale battles to set things aflame, or to rock the insurgent tree line with shrapnel. But I wasn't sure. My friend H would later tell me to keep a watch; if they fire too early you brake, if they fire late, you must accelerate. He was referring to rebel—or so-called bandit attacks—which sounded like wishful thinking, but it wasn't. And neither was it only Renamo rebels using rocket-propelled grenades on trucks.

Rolling past they patted their stomachs, showing that they were hungry. A split second later I was airborne, holding onto the steering wheel as the rig squashed over a huge trench. I shifted off the seat and into the side door with a mighty wallop. The rear-view mirror showed trailer wheels crunching into the pothole as I floored the brakes to no avail. Too hot from racing down the mountains, they weren't arresting the wheel drums any longer. Ripping up dust, driving became more daring on this winding, downhill road. Speeding was risky; smashing into the back of other trucks was common around here, but I was the only one on the road as far as I knew.

An older, light vehicle appeared on my left, stranded with a flat wheel. Bullets dotted the windscreen with spider web like holes. Nobody was in sight.

A few hundred meters later, a small, shirtless boy stood in the grass holding up a dead rabbit. I wasn't sure if it was an offer from the local bush butcher shop, or if he was just holding up his trophy for me to see.

Rumbling past a set of wrecks—two ten-ton trucks of East European origin—I slowed down for more potholes. Soon, they'd be removed—this meant dragging, or shoving them off the road to clear the way for traffic. There was no way of knowing the time of strike; tires can smolder for hours, even days, and both vehicles were burnt to a charcoal crisp. Half a kilometer ahead, another car appeared, followed by another small three-ton truck lying helpless in a charred, brown shell. This corridor was a graveyard of ambushes, a cremation site of bodies, now just ashes scattering in the breeze. Rusting wrecks and burnt out vehicles littered this road.

Slowing down for a narrow steel bridge over a river stream, a settlement appeared behind some trees. A few locals cheered from huts along the road. An old man sitting outside lifted his hand, taking forever to raise it in his greeting. The whole thing shook as I crossed. Hitting a stretch under a long line of trees, I saw the charred remains of a stranded minibus about half a kilometer ahead, well off the road. I couldn't see if there were bodies inside as I approached, and could only guess whether this was the rumored minibus from this morning's standstill.

A curfew had been imposed on this road, but its sentries, the soldiers bivouacked along the road were powerless. The unforgiving condition of these roads made it even easier for ambushes. Battling the sand and craters brought vehicles to a walking pace, which made them easier targets. If the vehicle in front of you was hit, it would be impossible to turn around. On this narrow road, a semi-truck had nowhere to turn.

Hitting the brakes, I slowed down at the sight of smoke. One of Brown's trucks—a South African operator. It had been burning for days, still rooted to the middle of the road. Twisted metal lay sideways over a heap of ash, and a track had been cut into the grass by trucks—one of many such deviations. Evidence of previously burnt-out vehicles already removed had been scorched onto clusters of tarmac.

I accelerated again, only to slow down after three hundred meters to zigzag around two more burnt out trucks, probably three-tonners. To an untrained eye, there was no pattern to these attacks. They moved all along the corridor. Any vehicle that wasn't torched had probably broken down very recently. Someone had mentioned that incendiary phosphorous grenades were used on vehicles that had come to a standstill. Those things were horrible; it's like napalm in a tin.

For a newcomer, this spectacle was as ghoulish as it was mysterious. Renamo weren't supposed to have bases here in the south. Their last one near Moamba, close to the South African border, was destroyed in the late 1980s. Later, we'd learn of at least one base in the Matutuíne district, near Ponta do Ouro, which was within hitting distance. Mozambique was experiencing a harsh drought and the rebels couldn't sustain themselves from the land, attacks and looting became more prevalent in 1991 and 1992. However, the culprits weren't that easy to identify. I'd heard that many of these attacks weren't coming from rebels, but freelance banditry. As time went by, I waved at government soldiers with less enthusiasm.

Further down the stretch, and already at high speed, another barefooted boy with a small goat appeared on the side of the road. I left his outstretched hand, begging looks, and torn clothing in the truck's wind surge.

A casual observation might conclude these bystanders oblivious to the proximity of the war, yet they weren't. Mozambicans I came across were undramatic in any expression of this conflict. Whether marginalized by the war, or desensitized from the prolonged violence, they all referred to it with a deceptive calm. The *Notícias*, the country's main newspaper, reflected only the party's will and views, controlling all coverage of military offensives.

The Mozambican press did not call this a civil war,

instead referring to it as 'the destabilization'. Renamo weren't called rebels; instead they were called *bandidos*, bandits. Sometimes it extended to *bandidos armados*, armed banditry. Attacks that crippled strategic infrastructure were seldom mentioned, or given much credence, yet massacres by Renamo were well documented and internationally publicized.

People in Mozambique referred to the civil war as '*a situação*', which translates to 'the situation', a term so common it could be mistaken for the official one. Indifference to the war was more remarkable than the tragedy itself. But here it was; the flames, the eerie smoke, the skeletal wrecks, the death and ashes. Seeing over forty such vehicles on every trip was a sensation that could be dizzying, like a narcotic. In the beginning it was a bit disorientating to find that many truckers were always cheerful and calm. There were no nervous jokes, there was no tenseness, or cautious tones in dialogues; I soon discovered that many smoked marijuana.

Reading the local newspaper for updates was a waste of time; the treacherous state of the transport corridors wasn't covered. In retrospect, they didn't have to; it was the accepted status quo.

I froze. Something had disturbed the stillness of the bush. Birds took instant flight, coming up out of the grass about one hundred meters from the road, behind a clump of trees. Scouring a nearby hillock for movement, vulnerability washed over me as my stomach tightened. Things were suddenly a little jumpy again; I was seeing ghosts.

Nearing Boane, I came upon a Russian T-54 tank stranded in the middle of the road. They didn't seem very effective against insurgency in this terrain; their new role seemed to be a personnel carrier. Approaching the green hulk of steel, I was being asked to stop by someone who really wanted my attention. Seeing soldiers huddled around aimlessly, I presumed it had broken down. Ignoring their stares, I diverted off the road, cursing beneath my breath when twisting axles caused a gear to grind in rejection. Clutch again, clunk, it went in. They looked on, bemused.

"*Então?*" So? A soldier called out with hands in the air as I trundled past. 'So' could mean anything, or nothing. So *Mulungu*, nothing for us today?

Their vehicle was likely out of fuel. It was common to see soldiers responding to an ambush going door to door in the local town, or stopping every passing vehicle for an urgent donation of fuel. This was always amusing, but not funny. I had seen the local garrison's Russian GAZ truck trying to push start this tank with a thick tire between the vehicles, and I had also seen the GAZ break down.

"*Então?*" I replied.

4 – Trophy

Two white truckers shot in Mozambique made news headlines in South Africa. It aired on SABC television's prime-time, and was plastered on all the front pages. The interest it generated surprised me. Mozambique was seldom in the news, much less anything to do with trucking.

H was waiting for repairs on his truck while he and Joe travelled together in Joe's International Eagle, with H driving. They'd been taking loads, part of a contract that H owned, on the 'northern runs' as we called them. After some late-night partying they woke up late, and missed the curfew as well as the armed convoy back to Maputo. Unlike the Namaacha-Maputo corridor, the military provided an escort on the national road north of the capital. But there were usually no return loads to loot. The assault on the 21st of March 1991 sounded like target practice for bandits.

Some inferred that Renamo was responsible for the attack, if that were so there was a degree of political intrigue. In 1984, South Africa and Mozambique had signed a non-aggression pact at Nkomati. The terms of the accord required apartheid South Africa to cease support for the rebels and for Frelimo to expel all ANC leaders from their country. Acts of sabotage, including planting bombs on civilian targets in South Africa, were being planned from Maputo. But both sides violated the agreement, and by the time South Africa had withdrawn any support for the rebels, it made little difference to the conflict. Renamo had gained enough momentum to continue their guerrilla campaign without external help.

I picked up the morning's newspaper, *The Star*, on the way to hospital. Judging by the pictures I expected to find my friends in a traumatic, helpless state, with a thousand-yard stare. H had phoned my boss, and asked me to bring his girlfriend—a lovely Mozambican girl who frequently travelled with him—along to the hospital. Walking beside her through the somber corridors of J.G. Strydom hospital, in West Johannesburg, deepened the melancholy. There was a thick stillness as we plodded through, followed by groans in the next ward, then more tranquilizer-induced silence.

"Clack, clack." The sound of my noisy brogue shoes invaded the hallway. Looking towards Vera ruefully, she replied with a faint smile over an air of calm. Just then we heard merry laughter coming from a distant ward and I saw a broad, bright smile develop on her face. I had to speed-march to keep up as she rushed towards the door.

"Hey, look what the cat dragged in! How's it, honey?" H greeted.

"Hello, gents." I smiled, watching H kiss Vera affectionately to hums and grunts of satisfaction.

"*Hoesit ou* Miguel?" Joe greeted in Afrikaans slang. We had walked into the tail end of some guffawing that had both Joe and H in stitches; you could see it on their faces.

"Hey, you've just missed some blokes from the press. *Jong,* we *smokkled* with their heads! They left here with their mouths gaping at our stories!" H chuckled.

The best way to describe H was the most colorful, effervescent character I'd ever met. Hendrik Fourie, or simply H, was affectionately called Haychy by other truckers. Good looking and nearing middle age, he bore the image of a white biker-rebel with a truck license. He had longish blond hair and steely blue eyes, with an iron will that was suited to the hard road.

I'd once spent two days with Joe and H on a farm. Afterwards, my stomach hurt from laughing at their antics, stories, and jokes. Towards strangers, H spoke normally, but around friends, he switched to a vernacular only he could have invented. Over years of trucking he'd created his own, unique jargon with quotes and phrases he'd borrowed along the way. A lot of what he said sounded humorous, sometimes poetic. Instead of saying 'I left that night', he would say 'then I drove into the sunset'. 'I was alone' was always 'I was the only stranger in town'. He'd say that 'it hurt so good', when referring to any woman he had loved. 'Winds blew through my mind' in place of 'I remember when…'

As time went by, he added Portuguese words, and catchy phrases he'd picked up in Mozambique to his vocabulary. This was aside from our South African slang which is peppered with Afrikaans words because they are so expressive. It gave a unique flavor to his special brand of story-telling, if one could understand it.

The flat side of the sheets on Joe's bed gave away an amputated leg.

"How far up was the damage, Joe?"

"Come check this thing out!" He called me over, lifting the sheets.

"Huh?"

"Check this thing! It's been stuck on growth mode for days now! I'm getting worried!" Joe said. He complained he had a permanent hard on, probably a side effect of medicine he'd been given.

"What are they feeding you here?" I asked, neither seriously nor frivolously.

"Too much love and tenderness, you must see some of the visitors we're getting!" H cackled with laughter, giving us a mischievous look.

I watched H's face change as the laughing died down; he was in constant pain. An armor piercing bullet had come through the clutch pedal and damaged his foot beyond repair. Before his own amputation, up to the knee joint because of gangrene, he was still waiting for a second opinion of doctors to asses if his foot could be saved.

"Are they giving you something for the pain?" I asked H.

"Ja, but these things have no effect. I told the quack to chop the foot off." I noticed Vera, sitting beside him, grimace, squeezing his hand.

The Star newspaper quoted Joe as saying, 'I saw my leg explode' when a bullet smashed into him. What he'd actually blurted was, 'Oh f**k! And I have just bought new shoes!' moments after impact, but I couldn't imagine reputable newspapers printing that. Although it was said in shock, and definitely aided by a bit of dope they'd just smoked, all the years I had known Joe, I had never seen him with new shoes. He once spoke of buying a pair of boots he saw in some cowboy movie. Mentioning a particular denim shirt and rawhide jacket, he spoke of it like it was an unattainable dream. Joe had always struggled financially due to his commitments.

The night before the ambush, was a typical Joe and H night out. Parked near the beach, H grooved away on his *bak*, his guitar, with a group of locals around a fire. Some danced, and others grinned merrily as he slammed out the sounds of Eric Clapton, the Eagles, and some blues under the palm trees. A joint in his mouth, he had them all boogying the night away. H's performances were captivating; his raspy voice and simple chords would enthrall anyone. He would say that 'during the war you'd drink and party with your worst enemy', something I only really understood later on.

"What happened, guys? Tell me the whole saga." I went on. H looked at me pensively for a few seconds.

"On that road back from Inhambane, about twenty kays north of Palmeira, you *mos* make out? There near Xinavane, I was telling Joe to roll us a *skyf*." He went on. For my own amusement I pictured Joe dropping half the stash on the seat while the truck rattled on the bad road. From a later recounting of this event, it's clear that they both had sensed a dark, foreboding hanging in the air that whole day. Their nerves were frayed by the time they'd left. A joint was the hell run's Xanax.

"What time was this?" I interrupted, looking at Joe.

"Don't know, late afternoon. You know *mos*, when the soldiers leave, the bandits move in. It was past the three o'clock curfew," he added.

H continued, "I heard these crackling noises, you know like that of a point two-two rifle. Then I see guinea fowl fly up from the bushes. I'm scheming who is here at this time of day hunting for guinea fowl? Like that's the first thought that comes to mind. Suddenly, I saw stones on the road. We were coming in at about a hundred and ten kays per hour; you could see that someone had moved most of them to the side. Next moment, I see little holes appearing in the windscreen and realize goodness, they are shooting at us!" There were three armed men in camos shooting AK-47's from the hip.

"We were out of there quickly. Man, we were deathly quiet for about ten minutes before H said, 'Jesus, Joe, we were lucky!" Joe added.

During the firing he actually screamed, 'It's Frelimo!' In this confused and frantic atmosphere, they didn't know who wanted them dead.

"Now, about nine kays down the drag we come to a bridge that is half blown up. You have to stop so that you can put half the wheels on the pavement. You know, the concrete side of the bridge, next to the railings, to escape the massive hole in the middle. You have to crawl through there. I was constantly looking in the rear-view mirrors as I maneuvered through this lot. As we came out of the bridge, there's this embankment on both sides. We couldn't turn around. When I looked up towards the road, there were about ten of them shooting at us a distance away on the rise ahead."

H paused to take a sip of water, coughed, then lit up a cigarette. He carried on with a bit more drama in his voice.

"Now, we didn't have a choice except to face it head on. I am changing gears up, up, all the time trying to break out. They were shooting a hundred meters from the truck into the ground, sweeping the firing upwards into the truck. Then this one stands in the middle of the road with an RPD. I check him aiming at the ground as the thing thumps away, then I check a line of bullets pelting the surface as that thing's kick lifts the gun. I see the direction of the bullets coming at us, so I swerve away from the line. Now, I'm swerving left right, bullets are shredding the dash and coming through the windscreen. We're only about a quarter of the way out and I hear Joe say, 'Oh, my God, my leg!' Now, I couldn't look at him. I am wet and sticky. I am just concentrating on getting us out of there. I say, 'Joe, don't worry, were almost out of it now.' But then, on the last one guy stands up and fires. As he fired, I felt my leg disappear beneath me and I fell behind the steering wheel. When I looked up, I was headed towards him. I turned the wheel, the whiplash of the trailer caught one of them, and I buried him under the trailer wheels. He looked like a piece of rag in the middle of the road." H paused. "Like a piece of rag." He stopped and looked at me with a frown, a hint of anger in his voice.

"The others are scattering, but from this side of the road, another RPD is pouring into us. I hear Joe mutter something just as I feel the heat coming through the clutch pedal on my foot. I am flooring the truck now. The bullets keep coming as I'm trying to see through the glare of sunlight reflecting on the cracks. So, I look in the rear-view mirror. It explodes… but we were out of range. Now I'm shouting to Joe, 'We're through, we're through!' There was blood everywhere. Joe was semi-conscious. I slapped him awake saying 'You're going to bleed to death!' I threw him a rag and told him to make a tourniquet. I couldn't feel the pedal. 'Keep your head, keep your head,' I kept telling myself. I started to feel woozy and just then the truck went off the road, into the bush before I pulled it back. The heat gauge is picking up steam from all the holes in the radiator, and all the warning lights are on now. So, I scheme to myself, we're gonna have run this thing until she seizes." H continued, taking a drag of a cigarette.

"Did she seize?"

"Ja, eventually. The thing groaned and spluttered its last about thirty to forty kays later. It's a miracle we even got that far. I looked at Joe passed out, leg dangling, and blood all over. I could see the bone. We were near a little village, so I opened the door and shouted for help. People were staring at us in shock. I passed out a while later before I could stop the bleeding. Man, I was dazed, ears still ringing and echoes from the gunshots. My head is planted on the steering wheel, then I hear the rumbling of a truck shaking the ground and think now we're goners."

A cattle truck from Xinavane stopped and four men—three blacks and a *mestiço*—loaded them into the back.

"We lay in our own blood. I was ice cold and my teeth chattered, then we went back on the same way we had just come from." Meanwhile, Joe had just come to, later saying of that moment, "A burning pain was eating away at my leg, particularly my thigh. I wanted to beg for something to dull the pain, but I couldn't speak."

Joe, realizing the direction they were going in kept muttering, "They're gonna shoot us! They're gonna shoot us!" thinking they were going to be dumped on that road and left to die. A few kilometers further on, the truck suddenly veered off the road and into the bush. Now it was H's turn to think they were being taken somewhere to be disposed of.

"My friend, we are about to die," he looked helplessly at Joe.

They were taken to a nearby Zimbabwean military base. Zimbabwe, Mozambique's neighbor, had sent six thousand soldiers to help protect the north-south highway.

"Please help us, we're badly wounded. We need urgent help," H begged the red-beret soldiers who thronged them.

There was immediate hope when the commander said they would radio Maputo for a helicopter. This was quickly dashed when they were informed 'radio out of order'—the battery was flat. H burst into tears as he heard. They were loaded back onto the truck, slipping and sliding on cow dung, to face a bumpy ride to a clinic in Manhiça. Both kept losing and regaining consciousness on the way there.

When they arrived, a Portuguese doctor who couldn't speak English, assessed that Joe needed an immediate blood transfusion as medics struggled to keep him alive. Through a Portuguese interpreter called Geoff, H was asked what his blood group was—O positive. Somehow, they established that Joe was A positive. They took blood from H and gave it to Joe.

After losing consciousness, someone saying, "He's gone", and more CPR performed, Joe was strapped upside down to keep blood flowing into his vitals, and a tourniquet was strapped on both knees and elbows. He died twice and was brought back again by two nurses.

H later described Joe begging them for morphine, which they didn't have, and swearing whenever they ignored him. There was nothing more this clinic could do for them; they had to go to Maputo right away.

"You know, Miguel, just before and during the attack, I was talking to God, just like I am talking to you." Joe continued, "*Broer*, I felt my spirit leave my body. [When I died] I felt this peace and calm. Travelling through this tunnel at a speed I cannot describe. Coming into this bright place all of a sudden, I sensed something was telling me I had to go back."

"What, like a voice?" I asked.

There was a pause from Joe. "I cannot explain. Almost

like telepathy. Then all of a sudden, I feel myself coming back into the confusion and pain crawling all over me. I scream at the two black nurses. I shout at them, 'Let me go!' I wanted to go back to the peace and tranquility." Joe looked at me with steady eyes.

Later, describing the events in more detail, H mentioned that a 'Frelimo commander, dark as charcoal', promised to escort them to Maputo because 'he liked South Africa'. There was some haggling over fuel for the ambulance before setting off that night with two armored cars escorting them. H never mentioned which, only 'you know, those Russian things with the big wheels'.

The medics wanted to load the mattress with Joe on it into the back, but it was soaked with blood. Their ambulance, with no equipment or medicine, wasn't in an adequate state to transport them. Adding to the drama, as they left town, they heard gunfire spitting out of the bush. After two retaliatory 'bursts of a 12.7' machine gun from the armored car the firing stopped.

With all the potholes and bouncing around on the road their wounds opened up, the vinyl seats filled with blood and became slippery.

"Joe's hair was caked in blood and he was almost unrecognizable." H explained later, elaborating that they had to sit on the floor, holding onto each other all the way to Maputo.

"*Broer*, no painkillers, nothing. I asked one of the soldiers riding in the front for one of my own cigarettes. He just laughed at me, puffing away. Love and hate *broer*, I tell you. Love and hate... I thought I would die again on that trip. Then we arrive in Maputo central hospital, you know the place, central of misery and dirt where people die in the corridors. They put us on some concrete slabs with about twenty people either dead or busy dying around us. My leg is developing gangrene, and they have no morphine." H explained.

Joe became delirious with shock. He kept pulling himself up on an imaginary rope, resembling a mental patient more than a wounded one, and still swearing at nurses. The medics did little. Other than some rudimentary words, neither Joe nor H could speak Portuguese, which became a big problem. They needed to get back to South Africa for proper medical care. After two days, a man brought his daughter into hospital and H overheard him speak English to her. In those days, before mobile phones with number storage, we all memorized important telephone numbers. H begged this man to phone Vera and explain their situation, which he did.

After visiting them, Vera rushed to the airport to look for an available airplane. She found two young, Afrikaans pilots who ran daily charters to Nelspruit on a bottom-winged Cessna. They agreed to help at little cost, as they were flying back empty on this return in any case. While the pilots removed the back seats of the plane, there was more drama in trying to arrange an ambulance, because Joe and H couldn't be transported by car. Getting the Cuban doctor to release them from the hospital was just as big a mission.

As they were dropped off near the airplane, the linen covers they had wrapped themselves in blew off. By this time, they had no clothes; they'd all been all been cut to stop the bleeding. There was no haggling from airport officials for documents—which they didn't have—once they saw how badly wounded they were. The pilot commented that Joe stank, that the smell inside the airplane was unbearable.

"Open the back window," he told him. In mid-air, not too low over the Lebombo Mountains their plane was shot at. I queried if these pilots had ever alluded to small planes being shot at in this area.

"I never asked them," H replied. I later asked Joe the same. "I was passed out, I don't know."

The only other incident I've come across was a single-engine plane from Netavia airlines doing an emergency landing on the Ressano road. It was a small repair and took off again shortly after.

They were forced to land at TSB Sugar near Malalane, because the left-hand wing had two bullet holes and the plane had lost fuel. After landing, they were taken to the Rob Ferreira hospital in Nelspruit and Joe was immediately operated on. Without time to take a breath, they were swamped by reporters and army intelligence before being transferred to Johannesburg.

"I have heard of blood brothers before, but this is incredible." I said, referring to the blood transfusion.

"Ja, we told the press we are now the heavenly twins!" H chuckled.

"Haychy, *broer,* if they chop that foot, we can share a pair of shoes!" Joe joked.

"Are you guys the same size shoe as well?" I asked.

"Ja, *swaer!*" H replied. We all paused, digesting the reality.

"Yah, that's tough, man," I said. "H, do you know who's responsible for this?"

"Ag, *broer,* they all say it's Renamo. I cannot say for sure."

"Did they have uniforms?"

"A mixture; some had jeans with a camo top, others

were wearing camos. Some were barefoot, some had boots. There were two adult guys in camos."

"What age where they?"

"Fourteen, fifteen, thereabouts."

"Who do you think it was?"

"Could be Frelimo; it could be opportunists. No telling, because uniforms can be stolen. You know that half the bandits don't belong to either Frelimo or Renamo."

"Any idea why they'd take out a rig that's empty, H?"

"Have you ever hunted birds? You know… the excitement of the hunt? I caught a look on their faces, you know, that glee of anticipation. You know that glee, that anticipation of the hunt. How should I put it? The crude excitement of the hunt!"

"What, like the truck is a big animal hunt?"

"Like a trophy, *broer*."

"Yah, I get the picture."

"The one almost shot his own foot off. They were amateurs. He jammed that trigger before he even took aim, so excited he was. The adults could have been there training this bunch as bandits, no telling."

"Yah?"

"They jumped out the way when I hammered towards them. But, *ja*, it was the excitement of the hunt. I think it's Frelimo dissidents training these kids. They are hungry, you know? What else have they got to do?"

"Yah, they're hungry."

A story of the terror trip was published in the *You* magazine in April. The modest royalties went towards recovering expenditures by Joe's boss, Louie, even though Joe was left without a job. There were no disability grants, or any other forms of compensation; they'd have to fend for themselves.

When Vera and a recovery team went to fetch Joe's truck, they were astonished. She counted eighty-seven bullet holes that had penetrated the front of the cab. The front rims, made of aluminum, were riveted to the brake drums with the number of bullets stuck between them. Tungsten-tipped ammo is designed to punch through armor plating; bullets were found as far back as the toolbox on the trailer. What was astonishing is that only three bullets hit them; one ripped clean through two bones on Joe's wrist and didn't feature in the whole saga. He bled little from this injury.

Vera helped H repair his own truck back in South Africa, like a mechanic and panel beater, overalls and all. Both drivers were trucking soon afterwards, sporting prosthetic legs—Joe with a right leg and H with a left one—sharing a pair of shoes. Incidentally, both were the same age, thirty-eight.

I had a nerve-racking experience driving with Joe months later. It had been raining heavily, and the rubber piece on the bottom of Joe's prosthetic, the peg leg, was wet and kept slipping off the accelerator pedal.

"F★★k!" The truck would jerk at the loss of fuel, then jerk into motion again.

"F★★k!" After some battling, Joe got the thing on rhythm only to miss the pedal again.

A few years later, a freelance reporter did a great radio documentary with H. It won a silver award with BBC radio from a series called 'truck tales'. Before they aired it on BBC Africa, H was sent a demo cassette, which I found very entertaining.

It started off in Johannesburg with a running commentary all the way to Maputo. At first, the conversation was quite laid back. She interviewed Vera, who was preparing their supper in the back of the cab's extension, and all was sweet. She was asking moderate questions at first. The trip continued, and H had a joint and a few beers. Then the documentary intensified; it drifted into a bar at the Buffalo Hotel in Hoedspruit, near the Mozambique border. It was 'National Woman's day', a public holiday in South Africa, and H was getting sloshed. At this point, it was undeniable that he was flirting with the reporter, trying to enthrall the wits off her. That's when she started asking probing questions.

The commentary continued into Mozambique and the topic turned to 'sex and Africa'. H explained how easy it was, how there's 'one' under every tree and so on. After being ignored for a long time, Vera was drawn back in with a question. By the way she replied, I could tell she had a bellyful of this. I shared my impressions with H, to which he replied that 'the freelance reporter was a professional, my *broer*, she edited all that stuff out.'

"Come, *ouens*, I'll play you a *kwaai* song." H said, dragging his guitar from the end of the bed.

"You *ouens* remember Jim Capaldi? Hey, long before Steve Winwood and traffic, talking about those years. He could slam a *bak broer*, those days before music with satanic overtures." H went on as Joe, Vera, and I waited.

H jammed, picking the strings like a man inspired. Joe sat up in his bed, eyes closed, humming to every rhythm, every note. It was captivating—something words cannot fully describe.

"*Olá?*" Vera broke the silence as the song closed with a dramatic, long wind down. A well-dressed man was standing in the doorway.

"Hum, yea, hum, hello." He said, followed by something like, 'Hum, I am from the so-and-so newspaper.' And suddenly, the mood was serious again.

5 – Timothy

It was too late to make it out of Mozambique. The curfew ended at 15h00, the border which was two hours away from Maputo closed at 17h00, and the dial had already clicked past 15h00. After offloading, most truckers would congregate here at the Praça 25 de Junho if we had missed the travel window.

On another humid afternoon I was rotating wheels, putting like tire threads alongside each pair on the trailer. When a tire burst, the thread on the spare did not always match the wheel in the same pair. I was always moving wheels around. With excess energy to blow off, I didn't mind the exercise. The locals sometimes referred to me as 'este boer nervoso', this edgy boer. It can be argued that I had an adult attention deficit hyperactivity disorder, which means that I couldn't stand still for too long. Those long drives, the purring of the engine, calmed me. And they couldn't always tell I was Portuguese—blue eyes aren't that common with us Latins.

Some drivers were having a discussion across the road, one of them making disparaging comments about me. At this stage, I didn't sleep in the truck when stopping over at the square and never hung out with any of them. His suggestion was that 'we give that cocky guy a hiding'; what feather-ruffling transgression I'd caused is still a mystery.

Timothy overheard the remark and stepped in amongst them to suggest that this wasn't a good idea, or something to that affect. He was the fittest looking guy around here, so they didn't protest.

Getting baked in the afternoon sun, I was perspiring with each snap of the wheel nuts as I pulled them tight with a power bar. Suddenly, the sun disappeared; someone was standing behind me. What now? More pestering from locals to *gimme me two thou for change da wheel*? You don't trust wheel tightening to strangers. Watching a truck wheel spinning past will convince you that it can write off a small vehicle on impact, or just cause a whole lot of trouble.

"Are you Miguel?" Said an unfamiliar voice.

"Yah?" I turned around to see a black man that reminded me of that great middleweight boxer from the 1980s, Thomas Hearns. Here was a Zulu with a grin on his face. The first thing you noticed about Timothy was a ripped torso and bulging muscles sticking out of a blue, short-sleeved shirt. He was impeccably dressed, a handsome man.

"H, he's my friend." He said.

"Ah... Haychy. And what's your name?" A wheel nut made a snap as I continued tightening.

"My name is Timothy. H said I must not come near you when you have a power bar in your hand." He joked.

"Sounds like H." I joked back, "Where do you know him from?"

"Zambia, Congo."

"Good times, heh? I've heard many a story about the runs up there."

"Are you going to Jozi?" (Johannesburg)

"Yah, but it's too late."

"We can go together, now." He replied. There was a

long pause; I wasn't in the habit of convoying with other trucks. I just didn't ride with anyone, full stop.

"We can make the border before five?" I asked.

"Yah, if we are fast."

"Ok, but we could get stuck at Namaacha. There's nowhere to park the truck there; it may not be safe."

"We will make it."

We punched holes through the traffic heading towards Matola. Plumes of exhaust smoke filled the air and honking vehicles pushed through narrow spaces, but we out-horned and out-muscled them. Tim's Jacob's brake dispersed of kamikaze pedestrians pushing wheelbarrows and trolleys across the tarmac.

We overtook a small truck whose misaligned axle made the vehicle drift sideways. The left front wheel rode on the tar, the rear left one on the sand. People were packed like sardines in the back of open trucks and 'chapa-cems'. I didn't understand what this meant; translated it means 'plate', as in zinc, or 'tin plate, one hundred'. They made up the local public transport industry, many with about a hundred people hanging from the sides, which may explain a hundred people on a tin. Most vehicles desperately needed an engine overall, as some of them were decades old and spares were as obsolete as the models. You couldn't help but have sympathy for these people.

Still, we cut through the congestion, forcing slow traffic that clattered along out of the way.

A policeman stopped a 125-cc motorcycle on the side of the road. We fast approached him as he inspected the rider's documents, his back turned to the road with one shoe on the motorcycle's foot rest. Timothy behind me flicked his Jakes as he rolled near him. The engine brake ripped from high revs, sounding like rolling thunder. Looking at my rear-view mirror, I watched the papers shake out of the policeman's hands; the jack-hammer sound must've spooked him.

Another policeman signaled me to stop. Just past Matola Rio, the road became a solitary lane before splitting back into two. The police had a habit of stopping vehicles at ridiculous places; in this case, just past the bridge where everyone slowed down for speed bumps. I pulled off into the sand; Timothy didn't. He remained in the center of the road, blocking all traffic behind us.

"*Documentos!*" Documents! He demanded. I didn't understand what documents he wanted, so I gave him a prolonged, dumb look. We were in a hurry and the border wouldn't stay open for us. If this was the usual time wasting, I'd already made up my mind, I'd spin away and let him chase me by foot. I handed him the first document I could find.

"No, give the certificate!" He demanded, obviously thinking I couldn't understand Portuguese.

"What certificate? Birth certificate, death certificate, which one?" I played along sarcastically.

"Yes, give, give!" He held out his hand. By now, there was a row of cars building up behind Timothy. The policeman's colleague across the road gestured with his hands, what's was going on?

"*Vai! Vai!*" Go! Go! The official pointed to the road. This guy, Timothy, had done me a favor.

Our two-truck convoy approached Boane, still making our presence known to slower vehicles. From the military checkpoint, just past the barracks on the other side of town until Namaacha, it was the corridor of death. The soldiers, normally found at the boom, had left. From here until the border, there'd be no military protection. We'd have to keep our eyes peeled for the slightest hint of danger— whatever good that would do.

As soon as we hit the corridor, rifle fire crackled in the distance, echoing through the bush. My stomach fluttered. We were already at high speed on this makeshift road of half sand and tar, yet I sped up instinctively. Goats and cattle loitered just out of Boane, causing us to slow down again. It was hard to tell from which direction the gunfire came.

Ratatatat...ratatat... An automatic rifle let off more bursts, dispersing the silence again. I looked at my watch, only to look at it again seconds later because I hadn't registered the time. A few seconds later, I realized that I still hadn't. It was late.

Vera, who was now travelling regularly with H, had mentioned that trucks had recently been held up in a queue at the checkpoint in Namaacha. A battle in the vicinity prevented them going any further. High caliber guns thumped in the distance, interspersed by mortar, or grenade blasts. She kept asking the soldiers at the boom what was going on, and kept getting 'we don't know' shrugs with blank looks. The officer's advice was to wait for vehicles coming from the opposite direction to 'find out what was going on'.

Ratatatat...ratatat. The firing continued, growing dimmer as we kicked up the dust. Coming across a streak of oil followed by bolts and pieces of metal in the middle of the road, I expected a broken-down truck at the next turn. For a kilometer and a half, there was no sign of a vehicle, then a burnt-out truck appeared—a ten-tonner blocking the left side. This must have been recent. By now, I'd memorized every wreck, every part of this road.

A quick look in the rear-view mirror showed that the truck's front portion looked mangled. Was it a landmine? How to know? Here tarred road became dirt again with islands of tarmac sticking over the surface; it was possible to plant mines here. As Vera's enlightened officer suggested, you had to be in the thick of the action to 'know what was going on'. There was talk that we should never step off the road; there were landmine victims in this region; how many was impossible to know. We raced towards the border, and Timothy was keeping up.

With increasing corruption within the military in the early 1990s, racketeering and gun running was coming from within their ranks. They executed a local commander in the Moamba region for attacking a South African convoy in early 1991, information I only came across years afterwards. That bit of news was selective; many South African trucks were ambushed and set ablaze in this period. I suspect there was much more of this going on as Frelimo cracked down on internal corruption.

We all knew it Renamo wasn't solely responsible for the attacks. Years later, an ex-FAM officer would tell me of hidden storages of goods looted from trucks by FAM. Even though it sounded like second-hand information it rang true.

There were many deserters from the armed forces which led to a rise in violent urban crimes. Some ninjas, the local slang for murderers and robbers, may have found their way to the transport corridors. These renegades had weapons and know-how of FAM operations, making them as likely candidates for banditry as any other group. There was also an incentive to move criminal operations to the bush. Urban vigilantism caught up with many of them by way of the 'necklace'. Mozambicans had learnt the art of 'necklacing' from the South African townships. It's a brutal execution—the victim's hands are tied; a tire is placed around the body then dowsed with petrol and set alight.

A common trait of all burnt-out vehicles was a lack of witnesses. Armed banditry seemed to prefer loaded trucks towards Maputo, but attacked vehicles in both directions, which eliminated looting as the only incentive. The advantage of riding back empty was speed and acceleration; nobody dawdled on this corridor. Sometimes you were attacked and didn't know it; excessive rattling from the bad road could prevent you from hearing gunfire. Only when you arrived at the truck yard back home did someone highlight pockmarks on the top of the container. When punctures were repaired, you found bullets inside the tire casing, and only then realized that someone out there didn't like you.

I had drama coming in on a previous trip. Rushing down the last descent of the mountain pass, the road curves to the right then levels out before becoming a long straight. At the end of that curve, I came across a semi-truck with a tarpaulin-covered load that had veered about ten to fifteen meters off the road. It had dug deep trenches into the sand when it ploughed into the bush. Only the tractor was burning, not the trailer, nor the load. But it looked suspiciously like someone had just torched it a minute or two ago. Flames were spiraling out of the cab; I could feel the heat and hear the crackling of fire from where I was.

A couple of soldiers stood in front of the truck. Perhaps there were more, but obscured from view, as I slowed down. One stepped forward a couple of feet, and excitedly signaled me to move on. I replied with a 'what's going on'

look and hand gesture, only for him to stare back with a
tight face, sending me away again. 'Go, go' his eyes
demanded. I wasn't sure what I'd just seen—a Renamo
ambush repelled by FAM, or they themselves burning a
truck? On first impression, it didn't look like it, but then
again, I was still trying to make sense of all this. When
you're on high alert, everyone's a suspect.

Only after a while did I pick up on why all truckers
brought about ten loaves of bread and a couple of cartons of
cigarettes with them from Swaziland on every single trip. If
soldiers pointed to their stomachs or showed you that they
wanted a cigarette, and you didn't throw it to them, *pasop…*
They would wag a finger at you, as if giving you a warning,
as if saying that your goods were in danger. My colleagues
often mentioned that their blood would run cold when
FAM stepped into the road as they approached. You just
didn't know.

Namaacha came into sight after rows of trees along the
mountaintop, marked by shops and buildings with fading
walls on either side of the road. Our immediate threat was
pedestrians who seemed unaware of vehicles passing through
town, so little was the traffic here. Two air horns blew in
synch as we entered a tired and ragged main street, down
shifting and shoving people off the road. As we slowed,
children chanted support in the local dialect; some ran next
to the truck with outstretched hands, all hoping to be
thrown back some reward. I caught a passerby glaring at me
before mistiming a hole in the road that sent the truck
airborne. Never, ever take your eyes off the road on
potholed roads.

The bankrupt town council had allowed these craters to
deteriorate so much, they could be mistaken for trenches.

Broken spring blades, damaged suspensions, and split tires did not deter the authorities from raising the road tax for foreigners—along with a 'vehicle movement' tax, import tax for vehicles, third party insurance, bribery for impeccably legal permits, and a fee for filling in your papers on undecipherable forms.

Coming to the end of the town, a small road market emerged just before the border control post. Rows of people stood around the boom. They were of the local bureau de change, waving wads of money, yelling at vehicles with filthy notes of ninety-nine shades of bacteria, printed on such low-quality paper that they would disintegrate after a while. Money agents offered to buy back the local currency you bought from them at a reduced price; the figure you'd see on the screen was sometimes from solar powered calculators which wouldn't function in the shade, typed on numbers worn off the keypad. Whatever... the Metical was worthless outside Mozambique.

During the war, everyone waved for trucks to stop, or cheered as you trundled past. It wasn't a time for quiet or unnoticed drives. Everyone approached you with business proposals, to bring anything from ostrich feathers to bicycle parts from South Africa. Because of international isolation, white South Africans were unaccustomed to dealing with foreigners, and Mozambique was breeding new entrepreneurs.

One naïve transporter brought in a whole load of potatoes into Mozambique. When he arrived in Maputo, the buyer of the load had no money to pay him. He landed up selling the load by the bag on street corners and markets. Braam brought five loads of cement for Maputo's chief of police, offloaded in the sheds at the railway station, but wasn't paid for the loads. Such cases of non-payment were becoming more common, which was more infuriating to hear, considering the dangerous road we travelled to get there.

I joined a small queue of trucks waiting to go through inspection for smuggling. A bored official stamped my passport as I approached his desk, without looking at my photo. The rubber stamp missed the target as it thudded down on the corner of the page, leaving a patch of smudged red ink. Being asked for a cigarette by a load inspector, I was told to go before I could open the container doors. Some kids slid under the wire fence that surrounded the complex, and ran towards the truck with begging hands, earning the last filthy Meticais I had. We exited Mozambique with minutes to spare.

Although its roads were fairly good, traffic through Swaziland posed further hindrances as well as many aggressive speed bumps. There was still a veterinary control and another military checkpoint to face. Someone once commented that if the Swazi military caught a foreign driver with a Swazi woman in their truck, they would lock you up. In Mozambique, we helped many people with rides on the corridors; driving through Swaziland brought on a very different mood. Although parts of it were beautiful and lush, there were miles of sugar cane plantations and our deadly enemies, the sugar cane trucks. They never gave way for overtaking and jumped out of dusty side roads without warning. Cane bundles were loaded precariously, sometimes hanging two meters away from their trailers. This nearly became the cause of another broken rear-view mirror.

We drove past a hive of trading along the road—stalls and shops lined up near the border. It was called Namaacha on the Mozambique side and Lomahasha on the Swazi side. Besides bulk, or staple foods, the two supermarkets with adjoining petrol stations never seemed to have anything interesting to sell. This next portion was the grey part of the route back to Johannesburg. Our two-truck convoy glided down the mountains as we headed into the haze that typified the sunsets here. The big orange fireball hung low and calm in the sky, setting the tone for the long drive home.

The mountain roads here were steep with a high ascent ratio. On the upcoming side, on any day, at least one truck's engines would overheat from the uphill strain; sometimes tires would lose traction on the ever-smoothening tarmac. Many trucks coming into Mozambique were far beyond the legal load limit, which made this climb toilsome. By now they had dug a track into the road, helped along by the sun melting the tar. It was cluttered with oil patches, blown seals, and a litter of bolts, nuts, and other pieces of metal trucks had shaken off. Manzini, near the Capital of Swaziland, to Lomahasha had been a gravel road until late 1986; this bad stretch with all the high climbs was seven kilometers long. What fun that must have been.

I once drove into a small oil slick here. A cold feeling came over me as the wheels spun before regaining traction. You needed an exit plan if a truck was incapable of handling these hills. A fully loaded semi-truck, if unable to come to a complete stop, will roll backwards. With our loads on this steepness, that was a likely outcome. Missing a gear on the down shift meant grabbing what you could, jumping out, and looking for a new job.

The mountain pass was a short series of S-bends, followed by another inordinately steep uphill, followed by another steep downhill. I'd once asked Braam, who travelled here in those days, how they coped with these hills before it became a tarred road; he only said 'you couldn't stop here'.

At the bottom, donkeys and cows threatening to cross the road kept you alert.

The sun kept dipping low in a purple, orange sunset as we edged towards Mananga border post and South Africa, the land of good roads with a very different ambience to Swaziland.

About a hundred kilometers into South Africa, just past the small town of Malelane, Timothy disappeared. I slowed down, looking in the rear-view mirror to see if he would emerge, but he'd gone on his own mission.

Night fell quickly from the sky; the world became black and white under a pale moon. The still of darkness took over here in the tropical region of the Lowveld as my thoughts hung. The monotony of the road and the engine's continuous humming could do that to you. All of a sudden, lights flashed behind me, flickering on and off emphatically. Seconds later, a familiar truck was riding alongside me; it was Timothy smiling through the lit cab lights of his tractor. He held up a packet of fried chips and a bottle of Coca-Cola, showing me that he'd bought us some food. Pull over, he indicated.

I trudged towards his truck at a layby we found, an International S-line with two chrome exhaust pipes sticking out the sides that gave it a macho look. As I approached the cab, I saw a dark hole of what looked like a bullet entry on the white paint job. I put a finger through it with child-like curiosity, pulling it out as I felt the shredded metal bite back.

"Where did you disappear to?" I asked, noticing that his cab was spotless; looking at a small dustpan and broom next to the passenger seat as I climbed up.

"Yah, I got food," he said, spreading out wrapping paper with fried chips and bread in the middle of the floor. I don't remember a black person ever buying me food.

"Thanks," I said taking a mouthful of chips. "So, you work for Harry?"

"Yah," he replied, putting chips in his bread.

"You guys run up north [of Maputo]? How are the roads up there?"

"Too hot, my friend." He spoke with a noticeable calmness. He took a bite of the bread-and-fries sandwich and spoke around the mouthful; "Last month, many people dead."

"Maybe you should stick to running only Johannesburg to Maputo," I replied.

"People die everywhere."

"I hear the war is different up north."

"Yah, but people are hungry everywhere."

"Yah," I replied. That was Mozambique's omnipresent word: hunger.

"You hear different stories. You go to Beira, they don't like Frelimo there. Maxixe, Masinga are very hot lately. I drove past plenty of cars and trucks taken out last week."

"What about the convoys, the armed protection up North?"

"You must pay money for protection. It's too much confusion with other vehicles. I prefer to drive alone. You hear different stories, but the road, hey, it can be bad."

"I hear that the war in the countryside, they chop limbs. They kidnap people, stuff like that."

"Yah, you hear these things. Some of them are Frelimo stories, some of them are true," he added.

As we talked, ate, and discussed the road, I noticed a

box of cassettes on the floor. Spending so much time behind the wheel made us eye any new music, occasionally exchanging cassettes with each other.

"You listen to country music?" I said, reading the names on the side of the cassette box. "Really?"

"Good stuff."

He handed me a cassette of Don Williams, a musician I had never heard of. I was more into blues, some folk, classic music.

"Ah, nice cowboy hat!" Looking at the cover I couldn't think of anything more intelligent to say.

We headed towards Johannesburg after supper. Mozambique, the hell run, everything that existed on that side of the border, had evaporated by the time we'd hit the halfway stage. Somewhere along the way, Timothy would disappear, but for now he was sticking behind me.

I pushed the Don Williams cassette in the tape deck. The dude was just too mellow; he was talking through his songs more than he was singing them. One, maybe two, numbers I kind of liked, but not the rest.

As we rolled on towards our destination, tiredness caught up and I fought the urge to sleep. Timothy flashed his headlights to see if I was nodding off. I responded by switching on my hazard lights. Yah, this dude was way too calm—Don Williams that is. This musical taste suited Timothy. He would tell you a horror story about carnage on the Mozambique corridors with the same cadence as reading a microwave manual.

6 – Unhitched

A thought dominated my mind: grilled prawns with *Peri-Peri* [chili] sauce. They would come after clams cooked in an exquisite sauce, complimented by delicious fresh Portuguese bread. That restaurant was at the end of a drive along the marginal, turning up at the Costa do Sol beach north of Maputo. Here, a small river joined the ocean, a pleasant walk during low tide that would always bring the sight of small crabs hurrying along the sand. It was an old building with fading white and blue paint, run by the same Greek family since the 1940s. A large balcony overlooked the ocean and parking lot, with hawkers and street kids begging from anyone who stepped out of a vehicle.

There was a small challenge though. I'd have to unhitch the tri-axle trailer housing nine hundred bags of flour, each weighing fifty kilograms. Including the weight of the container, it was almost fifty tons sitting there. Unhitching under these conditions was never a good idea, but neither was driving around with a trailer across town. If the parking lot was filled with cars, there was a risk of being unable to turn around. Costa do Sol was also a boundary; the furthest north civilians could venture along the coast during the war. There was no road beyond this.

Off-hooking—as it was otherwise known—the trailer

required heavy physical work, especially with 'slinging' down the thick landing legs. They had to be dropped onto a wooden railway sleeper, and the air hoses and electrical cable disconnected before the lever on the 5th wheel pulled, or disengaged. This is where a trailer's kingpin hooks onto the tractor's metal wheel. I'd seen truckers dropping trailer legs without using a sleeper, and after gallivanting on a jolly, they'd find it had sunk half a meter into the tarmac. This rendered it unhitchable, hanging too low for the tractor to reverse underneath the trailer.

There'd been a recent unhitching where the legs sank into the tarmac so far that the trailer's front kissed the ground. A burst water pipe flooded the road. They offloaded the trailer onto another two trucks, and that driver wasn't seen again. The government would later introduce a bonded warehouse complex called FRIGO just outside of the city, instead of allowing trucks to park in downtown Maputo and use it like a truck yard.

The engine hummed at low revs as my thoughts drifted along the palm-lined esplanade, and a welcome breeze rejuvenated me. Rodriguez, a Hispanic-American singer unknown in his own country, yet a cult figure in South Africa, provided the music for the hour. Simple, evocative acoustics accompanied his lyrics. He was to South Africans in the 80s and 90s what Bob Dylan was to Americans in the 60s and 70s. Growling in a nasal Hispanic voice he cycled between cynicism, irony, sarcasm, and brutal honesty. His words always touched a nerve. Words from a song about 'a dream', and 'the past' echoed in my head.

A picture of Rodriguez on the cassette's cover with his big, dark sunglasses, long hair, and dress was reminiscent of the hippie age. The music had a seventies feel to it, Maputo was stuck in the seventies, and it felt like the two had intersected. For a moment I was caught up in that era, and it felt strangely exhilarating.

In the nineties, a fan in South Africa created a website to begin an internet search for Sixto Rodriguez. He was eventually found in Detroit, Michigan, and invited him to play in South Africa. The muso had no idea he'd become a legend in South Africa. No one had heard of him in the United States, but he played to sold-out concerts in South Africa. Years later, when a Swedish filmmaker came looking for a story in South Africa, someone shared the incredible Rodriguez story. This swede made a documentary called *Searching for Sugarman*, the name based on the title of the first song on the album, *Cold Fact*. It won an Oscar for best documentary in 2013, but Rodriguez was asleep when it won; his daughter told him later. That BBC radio documentary H featured in was filled with Rodriguez music in the background, he doesn't know this either.

After supper I decided to go for a drive, so I took a detour along the Mau Tse Tung boulevard. I'd grown up in a time when whole families used to go for a drive for the sake of it. It was in an era when roads only trickled with traffic, and drivers weren't so emotionally revved up and impatient. Oh, the joys of seeing few other vehicles on your road, where you could drive all your restlessness away in the quiet.

An unusual sight piqued my curiosity, a group of street kids loitering outside the window of a little shop just off a side street. In Maputo, not many shops or stores were open for business; those that were appeared to be in vacant resignation with limited choices. Anything new had intrigue; even if you had plenty of money, there was usually nothing to spend it on. I parked the tractor across the road, and as soon as I jumped down the rig, I was accosted by street kids who were offering car guard services.

'Gimme Jorge one thou, me for look da truck.'

I waved them away.

It turned out to be a small art gallery. From the window, I could see two rows of paintings hanging on stands along the middle of the floor, a line of sculptures on the back wall. I was inquisitive, not that art has ever fascinated me, but I was wondering what any of these would sell for.

The first portrait I saw made my hair stand on end; it was a painting of one body with three heads. One had a look of horror, the other a wide-mouthed scream and the third face was covered in barbed wire. Pictures of pain, bondage, and confusion. I stepped away.

I walked quickly past the next painting of more agony and human suffering. It was if all these portraits were staring at me; fear and horror everywhere. It was stifling. There was an also undeniable sense that all these expressions were someone's reality; that the sorrow of the civil war had inspired most of this art. A picture—larger than the rest—showed a woman breastfeeding her baby with sorrow on her weeping face, but with a strange appeal about it. The next row was batik paintings which expressed a more mundane existence that toned down the mood.

"*Olá!* Can I assist?" Someone said in English with a Latin accent. I turned towards the voice. It was her; that girl I had locked eyes with months ago at the clube mini-golf.

"My, but these paintings are very impressionable. Some of them are like an open wound. Do you own this place?" I asked.

"No, it is from a friend. I am looking after it while they are away."

"Do you understand this art?"

"A little bit. I can find you a pamphlet. This here is Makonde art; this is a Shetani." She pointed to an ebony sculpture standing tall next to us.

"Ok, I must admit I am just curious. I don't want to give things names, otherwise I will have to take one home with me." The attempt at a joke using a simile of pets just came out sounding all wrong. She didn't understand.

"Yes, this art is only for some people." She smiled back.

"Shetani? Looks like a devil."

"It's spirits, animals." She said, pulling strands of her long hair back behind her ear as she blushed slightly.

"I have to admit that my understanding of art has always been of landscapes behind a blue sky, but mostly a pot with a bright, yellow flower planted in it." I said.

She smiled. Then we began to chat about trivialities until I pried a telephone number out of her. She seemed curious of this *boer* that spoke Portuguese. It was all reciprocal, for the few minutes we talked, her calming presence was the antidote to the images of barbed wire, screams and chains that left an indelible impression on me. On the way out, I noticed a few street kids still hanging about, the white of their eyes peering through the window, their noses rubbing against the glass. I could only smile.

On my way back to pick up another load in Johannesburg, I was excited to return, but the narrative of love and forever happiness never stays on topic. I gave someone a ride just outside of Nelspruit, seeing a white man hitchhiking was a rarity on South Africa's roads, especially at night. A concern for his safety made me stop.

"Where are you going to?" I asked.

'Witbank,' he replied.

As he climbed into the cab and smiled at me, I had to keep myself from grinning, because he had no front teeth. He was a fairly good-looking man, perhaps in his late twenties, moderately well-dressed, and well mannered.

"So, what finds you on a night like this in Nelspuit?" I kicked off the conversation as the truck pulled into the road.

"I went to Malelane to pay my last respects to my father."

"Ok. He died? When did he die? Sorry to hear that."

"Three years ago," he mumbled.

"And you could only visit his grave now?"

"Ja, I came out of jail last week."

"Oh." This was not unfamiliar territory. Having lived in 'certain areas', I had acquaintances on parole, awaiting trial, or about ready to go to jail. I kept bumping into drug pushers, guys up for housebreaking, car theft, and even armed robberies. One of them was robbing banks at nineteen. When his mother asked him where he was getting all this money from, he replied, 'Mom, I am robbing banks'. She thought it was a joke.

A week later when he was arrested his mother looked at his father and said, 'But he told me!'

Yah, I was used to running into criminals occasionally.

"So, what did you push time for?" I asked.

"Murder," he replied. My mind went blank, I had never met a murderer before, and wasn't sure where this was going. We left our firearms with the police at the border, and collected them when we re-entered South Africa, some defense against hijackers and thieves on these roads. But suddenly, that 45-pistol holstered on my right felt very cold.

"Murder? What, like killing someone?"

"Ja, I killed my wife," he said in a downcast tone.

"Your wife?" I wasn't sure if he knew this, but here in civvy street you didn't say that to strangers. Perhaps that's the way you started a conversation with a cellmate, but not with ordinary people. He continued without me asking him to.

"Yes. I used to be a security guard. One day I came home early because I'd forgotten something. When I stepped into the bedroom, she was with another man in our bed. In that moment, I picked up my 9 mil off the top of the dresser and shot them."

"What, both of them dead?"

"Ja, but I've forgiven her," he said with a vacant stare at the road. This guy had stumped me; I asked him what seemed to be the most obvious question.

"Are you sure it is not you that needs forgiveness?"

"The bible says we must forgive those that hurt us," he explained. "But, you know, in that moment... It was just in that moment. Even when her father visited me in prison... he said he probably would have done the same thing if it were him."

"Right..." There was a weird sincerity about him, and his 'in that moment' mantra sounded almost plausible.

"How did you lose your teeth?"

"The day I came out of prison. At Germiston station two blacks were robbing this girl. I tried to help, but got jumped by a few of them."

"Sad story..."

"It happens."

"So, how was prison?"

"It gives you time to think. It took me a long time to forgive my wife for what she did." This man was serious about forgiveness towards his wife superseding his crime; it piqued my interest.

"You really put forgiving you wife above everything else?"

"She was everything."

The truck rolled on into a dark night. A silence came between us as I tried to imagine 'in that moment', feeling a strange empathy for the man.

"And where have you come from?"

"Mozambique."

"Isn't it dangerous there?"

"Kind of, just bring your own minesweeper and bullet-proof vest. And yes, bring your own clean water, anything that kills mosquitoes, and don't get sick—there's no medicine. There's a war on the go."

"I have heard stories about that place. My dad used to go fishing there when it was called Lourenço Marques; he said it was like paradise."

"You can fish there, if there's anything left after the Russians vacuumed the sea."

"What happened in Mozambique?"

"It depends on who you ask, I suppose. It was a Portuguese colony for a few hundred years. There was a wave of black-nationalism sweeping Africa in the fifties and in the early sixties. Then a liberation movement, Frelimo, launched a guerrilla war on the Portuguese. The short version is that by the time Mozambique was given independence, most of the Portuguese had left."

"So then, what is the war about if the Portuguese have gone?"

"It is, well, a bit of a convoluted war. Frelimo supported other liberation movements with the same ideology. They were giving aid to Robert Mugabe's ZANU who used bases in Mozambique for forays into Rhodesia."

"What's a foray?"

"Attacks… Terrorist attacks, on missions, schools, farms. Anyway, so Ian Smith, remember him? The Rhodies used to call him Smithy. Anyway, suddenly with all the Portuguese out of Mozambique, he found himself with hundreds of miles of this new insurgent border to worry about. So, Rhodesia created a movement called Renamo out of disenfranchised former Frelimo leaders. They were trying to neutralize Frelimo, the Rhodies hoping this would force some political change in Mozambique. They've been fighting since the early eighties now, even after Rhodesia became independent. Then South Africa took over helping them, but not anymore."

"Who do you support?"

"Neither."

"Why?"

"It's complicated; both Frelimo and Renamo are bad. Things in life don't always fit nicely into the good guy, bad guy thing… You know, into nice little wrong or right boxes. Maybe even like your story?" I went onto explain to my audience that it was Frelimo's own atrocities that drove some to Renamo. Yet, Renamo had evolved into a destructive force that brought misery upon Mozambique.

"Are you following?" I probed.

There was no response. He was lights out, snoring, head tucked into the headrest. He was probably overtaken by exhaustion after spending the whole afternoon in the sun trying to get a ride. Perhaps my over indulgent explanation of the conflict had put him to sleep.

Facing the night, the truck's engine droned along a lullaby as I pondered this man sleeping in the passenger seat;

his future, and his concept of forgiveness. I thought about how much he must have loved his wife, but especially about that 'in that moment' thing. And how his unhitching had worked out.

7 – Saboteur

August 1991

R olling into Lomahasha I knew there was no getting into Mozambique today. I'd been delayed from entering Swaziland from South Africa because they'd changed the criteria for permits overnight. To transit the country a prepaid bond for the value of goods was mandatory, and a lot of forgeries using legitimate bond numbers were doing the rounds.

"They won't let you through, it's too late," the Swazi official said. The round, wall clock in the office showed 16h55.

"I can't turn around and I'm not sure how safe it is to park here at night. I could wake up with tools and wheels missing," I appealed.

"See, a police station?" He pointed outside the border gates "There's someone else in the same situation as you. You can also park in that space." He pointed to an area between the two countries, in no–man's–land.

"It's fenced off," he continued.

"Ok, thank you." I rushed out and still tried to gap it. The Mozambican officials at the boom had other ideas and signaled me to reverse. I maneuvered next to a new blue-and-white Scania 142H cab over with industrial machinery loaded on a tri-axle trailer. For the first time ever, I'd sleep over in Namaacha and wasn't happy about it.

My truck was still idling when I heard a knock on the door. I recognized Willie straightway. He was an ex-colleague from a previous trucking gig.

"My goodness! Of all the people I didn't expect to see."

He smiled back. Willie was a young, blonde-haired South African, soft-spoken and likeable.

"It's good to see you," he replied.

"Hey, get inside," I invited, leaning across the cab to open the passenger door. It rocked as he stumbled in and made himself comfortable. Truckers have this habit; the first thing they do is scan the cab, then study the dashboard, the seats, the bed, the whole thing—comparing it to theirs.

"How's this Volvo?"

"Most comfortable truck I've ever driven, although this thing's diff ratio is wrong. It will do bullet speeds on a downhill, but the lower to mid-range is not optimal. Also, it's very quick on a straight."

"What engine?"

"380 Intercooler."

"How long have you been coming to Moz?"

"Best part of a year."

"And how is the road to Maputo?"

"It's bumpy in many places, lots of potholes. Be careful just after the town; you're passing close to other trucks on some killer downhills."

"I meant the shooting up of trucks."

"Oh, hum. So, so," I replied wiggling my hand. "Not hot, not cold. Sometimes a few vehicles get taken out on the same day, then it's quiet for a couple of weeks." I turned towards him. He seemed lost in thought.

"So, how is that hot babe you were dating?"

"We're married now."

"Congratulations! This trucking thing not getting in the way?"

"We get by."

The conversation drifted into stories about trucks getting stuck, which loads had challenged us and the insane tonnage my boss made me load.

"So, what are you carrying?" I asked.

"Some machinery and a forklift."

"Forklift, hey? That reminds me of a story Joe told me about Zambia." I recounted a mildly humorous story Joe had shared with me. It may only have been my perception, but he seemed a little tense about this Mozambique gig; I was trying to keep things light hearted.

"So, everybody knew each other on the Zambia run. One morning, two friends stopped in a queue at the border. Seeing there was no movement in the truck in front of them, they woke up the driver for a cup of coffee, or something like that. They were greeted with cursing and swearing from the guy inside who didn't want to get up any earlier than he had to. At this stage, this driver was still lying in his bed. But now he's awake, so the one guy outside the truck asks 'where are you going to?' And the other one asks him 'and what are you going to do there?' The reply was something like, 'what do you mean what am I going to do there? I'm going to deliver this grader!' said this irate driver. So, one guy asks him, 'what grader?' To which the driver replies 'the f*****g grader that's on the back of my lowbed trailer!' The other guy replies, 'but there's nothing on the lowbed…!' To which the irate driver replies, 'ah, bulls★★t!' So, the guy tells him to come and see for himself. Eventually, a bleary-eyed driver appeared in the window with an obvious hangover. He jumped down the truck and realized that these two guys weren't joking. A day later, they discovered the tracks of the grader in the bush. It was still on its wheels, just the canopy was damaged."

Willie scanned his trailer to see if his machinery was securely tied down. Instead of taking his mind off the run, I may have made him jumpy about his cargo landing up in the bush.

We spoke for over three hours, which sent me into yawns. Nearing 21h00, I lay on my bed reading a book by Aleksandr Solzhenitsyn, *One Day in the Life of Ivan Denisovich*. I read one paragraph before falling asleep; it had been a long day and I was lights out. A bomb couldn't have woken me up, so to speak. The next morning, at about 6h00, I pulled the truck's curtains. Seconds later, I heard a tap-tap-tap, a knocking on the door. Willie was standing outside.

"There was a lot of shooting last night, many blasts. Did you hear it?"

"Huh?" I replied still rubbing my eyes awake. "Say what?"

"Shooting, a lot of shooting last night, lots of explosions." He sounded nervous.

"Are you serious?" I asked. What I was thinking was, 'It's the guy's first trip into Mozambique, he thinks it's Stalingrad out here in the sticks.' Then I asked, "Do you have any coffee? I'm out."

"Yes, I've just made. I haven't slept all night." He hurried towards his truck to get a flask.

The Namaacha's border office was operating as normal. At first, I never inquired about the previous night's supposed commotion, still wondering if Willie was a little delirious. It turned out that he wasn't.

Two Portuguese guys on their way to Swaziland mentioned an attack by Renamo on the town. On first impression, it seemed exaggerated, probably because they were so calm about this *situação*. After clearing the load papers, I beckoned Willie who was still waiting in his truck for clearance, and he waved back at me. 'See you later?' I haven't seen him since.

I idled down the main road that cuts through Namaacha, rolling slowly through the town. The collective mood looked subdued, the customary waving and staring at trucks with interest was missing. The hotel Pequenos Libombos on my left had been revved; all its windows were shattered, bullet pockmarks dotting the lime green building. Another building near it had clumps of wall gouged by machine gun fire.

This was only four hundred meters from where we'd slept. Two standing trucks would have made good targets; a wire fence wouldn't have stopped the rebels had they ventured that far. I saw a few other buildings shot up, razed with gunfire. According to later discussions, I heard that the rebels had run through the town and emptied magazines on 'anything that moved'. They fired rocket-propelled grenades into specific targets, anything that represented the state.

It had been a while since Renamo had attacked Namaacha, they couldn't hold towns and they must've had objectives other than wanton destruction. They were known to target clinics, kill people in hospitals, and kidnap doctors and nurses. It may also have been an effort to shore up their own shortage of medicine and medics. This was one area where Frelimo had some success due to donated medicine, along with equipment and foreign volunteer medics.

Another likely reason was a lack of food, because of the drought. Namaacha bordered with Swaziland which had an abundance of supplies. The rebels' modus operandi was to kidnap people to act as porters for what they looted, and hide the spoils in mobile bases. By the sound of things the assault had lasted for a while before FAM repelled the rebels, which reminded me of a chat I had with Braam,

"During one of my first trips around the end of '85, perhaps the beginning of '86, Frelimo [FAM] had just killed six or seven Renamos. There as you come into Namaacha, just after the border post. They left the bodies in the street," he went on.

"Like an exhibit?" I asked.

"Ja."

He knew the Namaacha-Maputo road better than anyone else. As I sped into the corridor, I noticed that soldiers, who normally bivouacked along the road, were absent, which felt eerily similar to what he'd mentioned. "There was little wildlife near this road in the eighties. This road had a deathly, haunting silence."

Probably the first South African truck to be taken out on this stretch of road was driven by Simon Mtweni, one of Braam's drivers. That was back in 1986 when our trucks were a rare sight, and FAM's presence on the road was non-existent. A group bandits stepped onto the road and opened fire; one of the tracer bullets ripped through the windscreen, hitting Simon on the cheek. Dragging him from his truck, they forced him to carry bags of sugar and boxes of blue bar soap out of his own load deep into the bush. They stuffed his cab and trailer full of dried shrubs and grass then set everything alight.

(I'd also heard of bandits shooting fuel tanks, although

diesel isn't flammable; it is combustible, which feeds an existing fire.)

Simon was later freed, walking many kilometers back to the road to pick up a ride. According to him, had he been a Mozambican or Swazi driver the bandits wouldn't have left him alive. In the mid-1980s, Renamo seemed to be more about looting trucks than killing drivers and their passengers, but that changed over time. Braam's adage was that 'Frelimo wore boots in the day and walked barefoot at night'— barefoot referring to banditry. Another take of his was that Frelimo had reason to eliminate witnesses; survivors were of some propaganda value to Renamo, but anathema to corrupt *militares*.

FAM sprayed chemicals to kill trees and plants alongside the road to limit bandit concealment, but that turned out to be a failure, he further explained. Of all the things he mentioned there was one detail that I probably wouldn't have noticed or ever known about. The majority of attacks, and burnt-out vehicles were on the left side of the road going towards Maputo. The right-hand side of the road had been mined by Renamo, only they would have known where. Banditry always appeared from the left.

A peculiar incident occurred towards the end of 1986. As the road straightened out after the Lebombo Mountain slopes, about seven, perhaps eight armed bandits stepped onto the road. Coming in at a considerable speed, about a hundred and fifty meters away, he noticed that they suddenly froze. It seemed as if, in his own words, 'They were taking orders from someone, then turned back into the bush like they'd been told to'. Asking if he had any further insight, Braam gazed at me through his spectacles and said, "It could only have been God protecting me."

"In those days, back in 1985, I was the only transporter coming here," he went on. "I brought loads for Interfranca who supplied the embassies in Maputo. On my first trip, when I parked my truck in Avenida 24 de Julho, I was the only vehicle on that street. All the shops were boarded up, there was nothing to buy. Sometimes, I couldn't fall asleep, and there was sporadic gunfire coming from different parts of the town. The whole country had an uneasy vibe. In those days, there was a single, functioning restaurant in Maputo. There were hardly any vehicles, no traffic, and few people in the streets."

Things had changed from those days, but when I first arrived here, they were still jumpy. On my second trip back in January 1991, I was still unsure of what to expect from this gig, and didn't know anyone here. I met another transport operator at the customs square whose name was Johan to the best of my recollection. He was a big, burly Afrikaans guy who happened to be coming into Mozambique for the first time.

We unhitched his tractor and went to that restaurant in Costa do Sol for supper and chatted for two hours. It was the middle of summer; we were dirty, hot, sticky, and craving a cold shower. Driving back along the marginal, the sea embankment, I had this bright idea of 'let's take a dip right here'. Near the Clube Naval, there was a metal railing leading into the water. We parked the truck and went for a swim. As we came back out, onto the sidewalk, two policemen stood waiting. Click-click, there was a cocking of an AK-47 rifle pointing at us.

We needed to go to the *esquadra*, the police station, they told us. I, being the Portuguese speaking one asked why. Out came some incoherent accusation about *sabotagem*.

Turning to Johan, I explained that we were suspected of being saboteurs coming to assassinate the President. Apparently, the residence of Joaquim Chissano was on the hill overlooking this side of the seafront. Johan gave me an incredulous look before breaking into hysterical laughter, now it was the turn of the police to look stupefied.

I was trying to clarify the situation with my captors, and the longer it wore on, the more convinced they seemed that we were frogmen. With all their blathering, it was hard to tell if this was leading up to a bribe; it may have just been an inability to reason on their part. Probably having been warned of a threat from the sea, and believing the hype, they'd become heroes that thwarted an assassination attempt.

I asked them if they had noticed that the *boer* next to me had a huge pot belly. Although I was, my companion was in no shape to swim more than a hundred yards. Fortunately, Johan didn't understand. Then I asked them why—if we wanted to kill the president—would we come in from the sea if it was much easier to come in via the border, you know, by car, or truck? Seeing no blink in their eyes, I gave up reasoning and said, 'Ok, take us to your *comandante*, maybe we can talk sense there.'

And… how are we getting to the *esquadra*? They explained that they had no transport, but would escort us there, in our vehicle. I explained this to Johan, who didn't know if he should laugh anymore, but now I did, chuckling hard. We took out some money from the Iveco tractor and told them to buy themselves some *refrescos* before they could argue any further, and thanks for the laugh. Still, they wanted to arrest us and we just ignored them; they'd already taken our donation. That's the last time I saw Johan, but not before he'd stressed that it was the funniest thing he'd ever been accused of.

I have since learnt that landmines exploded on the beach in 1986, and attacks on the suburbs of Maputo were common in '91 and '92. In the 80s, there was an attack by South African Special Forces coming into the bay on inflatables. They found the target house with ANC operatives near the seafront, but unfortunately went into the wrong room and killed innocent people. If suspected of being a spy or saboteur, nothing less than solitary confinement or execution awaited you. Had we been aware of this, we may have taken the whole thing more seriously and not laughed as much. That wasn't the worst of it; locals told me that sharks were also frequent visitors to the area we swam in.

Next to the customs square on the Praça 25 de Junho, the Fortaleza de Maputo, a quadrangular fort built in the 1870s, overlooked the bay of Maputo. The original cannons protruded from gaps in the thick, red sandstone walls. Once used to keep invaders at bay, it was in good shape, literally a museum. Down below, in a dark dungeon-like section a water pipe was sticking out of the wall. For a fee, the gatekeeper would turn on the tap to let you have cold shower—something almost as exhilarating as the saboteur thing. After meeting Cuca I was upgraded to a modern shower with soft towels and body lotions, but those creature comforts lacked a certain thrill.

Early the next morning at the square I jumped down from the cab, leaving the passenger door open while a John Lee Hooker song blared though the speaker. I brushed my teeth discreetly next to the water tank fitted to the side of the truck. Feeling a strong human presence around me, I reasoned that this wasn't unexpected on a public street. As I turned, flicking the water off the brush, there were half a dozen street kids dancing around the truck.

Boys who were the product of poverty, displaced, or abandoned through the war were grooving to the boogie, hopping and bopping around the cab. One's funny adaptation looked more like Kung Fu than dancing. Another kid, about eight, bare-chested with a running nose, looked like he was mimicking an airplane. They danced, laughed, and chortled through the whole song. It wasn't about begging or asking for anything, they just liked the song.

8 – Lonestar

On one of my last trips into Mozambique, I had a near miss. Tearing up the road as the Lebombo Mountains began their wind down, Creedence Clearwater Revival played a hypnotic and drawn out rendering of '*I heard it through the grapevine*'.

Oozing with calm, the day had small fluffy clouds drifting in a gorgeous sky, a contrast to the treacherous road below. The brakes, struggling to slow the truck, backed off as I let it roll. With these overloads, brake drums can get red hot and set wheels on fire. After a while they develop severe crack formations from excessive heat; if not replaced, they will shatter and disintegrate. Another trucker I'd come across once saw pieces of drum metal shooting through a car's windscreen behind him—luckily no one was hurt.

Cutting and weaving through the dense bush, this decrepit road was making the cab shudder. There were stretches of remaining tarmac where I could pick up speed, but elsewhere, the road felt like it'd shake the truck apart. It was a chiropractor's delight.

An obstacle appeared.

As the mountains flattened, I caught a glimpse of a blue, rusting forty-foot container atop a two-axle trailer. It disappeared quickly behind the tree line. Half a kilometer of more cheating on your partner melancholy coming through the speaker, I was within range of a dust cloud.

Down shifting, I looked for a gap to overtake, which was nearly impossible under normal conditions. Catching me by surprise, the trailer's one working light glowed dimly red beneath a dusty lens. He was stopping hard. My brakes were too hot… I veered right to avoid running into him, lining half of my wheels into the bush. Long grass concealed a bumpy surface; the top-heavy container tilted the trailer as it ploughed the earth. Digging up chunks of grass with the bull bar, I rammed the stick shift, feeling the crunch of gears biting back. The momentum was carrying me as I passed alongside him. I'd come across this tractor before; it was an old, single diff Mercedes 1924, a Mozambican *skorogoro*.

A truck length away, I glanced at my rear into a mirror that was seldom wiped clean. At night, cars approaching from behind had an annoying habit of throwing their high beams at me when overtaking. Leaving a layer of dirt on the glass limited the glare, but now it limited my view, I couldn't figure out what was going on behind me. Further obscured by the dust being lifted, all I could see were shapes of men moving in front of the ivory colored bonnet. Had I unwittingly just used this truck as cover to get past an ambush? An odd sensation came over me, where the truck was standing still and the road was moving around me. I was suddenly aware of every detail, every smell—of the slightest movement around me.

The stereo droned on.

Vera once remarked that the one hour stretch between Namaacha and Boane took more out of you than driving twenty-four hours non-stop. From someone acquainted with the runs up north—which were toilsome and emotionally draining—it was saying something. It would explain why I was always exhausted when arriving in Maputo, this stretch of road was always an adrenalin rush without you being aware of it.

Being shielded from an attack on the left had happened before, in a manner of speaking. Petrus, a black driver riding a white Ford Louisville, drove into an ambush somewhere between the quarry and the area of my incident. Coming from the opposite direction, he'd given a woman as well as a soldier a ride from Boane. When the bush came alive with gunfire the woman was hit in the breast, the soldier opened the door and retaliated, firing blindly with his AK into the bush. He was hit in the head. Petrus was unharmed. After losing all its water and oil, the engine seized a short distance past the ambush. Even after it had stopped, he was still flooring the accelerator, so frightened was he.

A passing van, or pickup, coming from the Namaacha side stopped and took both him and the woman to the border. But Petrus' trailer had closed off the road, which forced Daniel and H who arrived soon afterwards, to stop. Hearing the angry crack of AKs, they ran into the bush and crouched. While bullets snapped overhead, H found a group of soldiers hiding, disorganized, and reluctant to do anything. He ran—or rather, wobbled—on his peg leg towards his truck, fetched a bottle of whisky and 'jammed it down their throats'. Those were his words, which was his way of saying that he talked them into taking swigs for instant bravery. Then he gave them a fiery speech, trying to rouse them into action. Those are his words too, which meant he was swearing at them in rapid fire Afrikaans, English, and Portuguese cuss words all at once.

Twing! Twing! Bullets were hitting their containers, but with so much tree cover and foliage, nobody seemed to know where it was coming from. The soldiers eventually kicked into action, but didn't look all that fearsome. They ran, firing wildly, hoping the noise of their guns would scare the enemy. At least, in the way it was described to me, that's what it sounded like.

It wasn't uncommon to see government soldiers in the vicinity of a hit. Before my time here, Jannie from JH transport was speeding along in a pickup towards the border when he saw thick smoke billowing ahead. Recalling the incident, he couldn't remember the exact area, but a comment of 'seeing soldiers on a hill next to the road' pointed to one spot. Just after the scattered, dilapidated buildings near the quarry the road veers hard right and descends into a big dip. There's an imposing hillock on the right, the most likely location. He thought of stopping near them, but his colleague insisted it wasn't a good idea. Up ahead, two trucks had been ambushed. A green Oshkosh driven by Kortman, a white driver, riding in front was shot full of holes, but managed to get past. The Louisville behind him was burning; the driver Robert, who was shot in the arm and in the leg, was picked up and taken away.

There were many anxious moments on this road, but what terrified me most was Artur's driving. My initial interview for this job wasn't made up of the usual background questions and a test drive. Artur, a short, bearded man, and devilishly good-looking, sat in the passenger seat as we headed out together. My Portuguese boss would have enough time to assess me; Johannesburg to Maputo was over nine hours away. I'd never handled a Volvo gearbox, but was used to ZF gearboxes with the ecosplit function of other European trucks. The tonnage and top-heaviness of the container was a challenge, with the extra concentration tiring me quicker.

Saying little until the other end of Swaziland, he took over the wheel at Namaacha. The way he threw the truck around on the Lebombo Mountains had me clawing holes into the seat. It was his way of saying that on this road you have to drive the rig like it's stolen, or as if you are being chased by a leviathan. His fast cornering tilted the container to what seemed like twenty degrees at places. After a while, I avoided looking in the rear-view mirror to keep my anxiety to a manageable level.

I hadn't seen Maputo in seventeen years; I thought I'd never see it again. Artur neglected to tell me that this gig was dangerous, seeing heavily armed soldiers on the road was the first hint. He'd also forgotten to warn Joe who did a single trip for him in 1985 in a Volvo G89. With little traffic passing through at the time, he didn't see any soldiers protecting the road, after blowing a tire he thought nothing of changing the wheel immediately. A warning from a passing car saying 'you must move, they kill people on this road' was the only clue he got. Braam was just as oblivious, it was only after the recovery of his first burnt-out truck that he realized the gauntlet he was running.

Nice vistas and an easy-going atmosphere in the capital seemed a world away from the conflict. As the country muddled through, I'd had a fairly enjoyable time for the last year. Occasionally, we'd go to *feira* for exquisite peri-peri, barbeque chicken, or to hang out at some *buraco* with friends. When really bored, I'd visit the *Bazar da Baixa*, the noisy central market, to watch women shout and see smelly fish twitch on tables. Built in the early century, it had a characteristic colonial design; it also had cashews, spices, produce and perfume from 'Paris'.

On some weekends, my girl and I would go to a racing stadium near the beachfront. Seating about two thousand people on the concrete stands, I'd watch cars that looked like they might've been stolen in South Africa spin off the track. When nothing else was on, I'd read books, sometimes go for walks on the beach with her, and watch the gentle waters of the Indian Ocean hugging the sand. I'd watch a silhouette of fishermen heading towards their boats for a night watch. At night, the beach looked deserted, but it wasn't; street kids would often sleep in the trees for safety. We'd always run into police, and she'd always have to say, 'Calma, calma,'—don't fight with them. I always did.

After the turnaround of my final trip, I waited in a queue at Namaacha's passport control. With nothing else to do except twiddle thumbs for a few minutes, something piqued my interest; a faded poster on the wall next to me was imposing itself. It was of Mozambique's national flag, the only one in the world with an AK-47 on it. For once, I was up close to one, and for once, taking notice of the detail. The rifle was crossed with a hoe at the forefront of an open book which represented the liberation, agriculture and education, all centered over a star of communism. I knew none of this, so I had to inquire later, but my first impression was that it represented bloodshed. Das Kapital and famine. Technically I wasn't wrong.

Until recently, any opposition to the state's political doctrine or challenging the inerrancy of the party landed you in jail. Corruption and abuse of power had characterized them more than their struggle against colonialism. Common people didn't actually rule, but were expected to show obedience and loyalty to this system. But the symbol that wasn't on the flag was Frelimo's mass killing of dissidents after independence. A hundred times more lives than the struggle had cost.

"Ma friend! Ma friend!" A kid stood next to the truck as I walked out. His outstretched hands came with the best underprivileged look I'd seen, his head cocked sideways in overemphasis. An elderly man chided the boy, chasing him away, now smiling at me as if he'd done me a favor. The kid stopped a distance away with a mischievous grin. I chuckled. As I rolled past the boom on the Swaziland side, I looked back at Mozambique disappearing one last time. The rear-view mirrors were still a haze I noted.

Hitting the Witbank highway, now well into South Africa, I pushed the Don Williams cassette I'd borrowed from Timothy into the tape deck. One song caught my attention, something about a hero that saved a girl then rode away. I resonated with the part about getting back to her one day, but we hadn't even kissed yet. Johannesburg was only two hours away, what a 'Lone star state of mind' meant I didn't know, but it seemed to describe me on the final stretch home.

As the monotony of the road wore on random thoughts circled my mind. Recalling the 'in-that-moment' hiker I mused on how long a moment actually was. How long can it last? Gosh, I was tired. The truck would roll and my mind would wander with it; sometimes my thoughts would feel like they were stuck in gear.

Sometimes they'd drift to another era, when times were so happy; to when I first left Mozambique. I was only a child then. It's a place where memories come to me so effortlessly. That flight to South Africa from the country of my birth was via the Ressano border; I remembered it like it was yesterday. It was a beautiful day when we left, the heat percolated through that yellow Alfa Romeo GT without air conditioning as my family headed to South African for a new future. We were the fortunate ones.

9 – Flight

The upheaval in Lourenço Marques, September 1974

Shouts of protest in the streets below us interrupted the morning. I was lying on my bed reading a Tintin comic book, enthralled by his mythic adventures around the world when I heard the tumult. As a boy of eight, I was so captivated by this story that nothing seemed capable of distracting me from its narrative.

As the commotion outside drew closer and grew louder, so did the adventure come to an end. Peering towards the street five floors down I saw a large crowd, made up mostly of Portuguese men and women. They were marching in demonstration along Avenida Nossa Senhora de Fátima, parallel to the army barracks.

We lived in Bairro da COOP, a cluster of high apartment buildings lined up along the main road. About a twenty-minute walk from the sea with a peripheral view of the South and East of Lourenço Marques, the capital. Up to now, public dissent had been largely out of sight; now it was on our doorstep. This demonstration was a part of the September revolt, the Portuguese Mozambicans against the Portuguese government. Lisbon's decision to hand over power to the Frelimo rebels, the signing the armistice on the 7th of September with no consultation of Mozambique's people, was unpardonable.

Grândola, Vila Morena

The events of 1974 came at us fast; it was a confusing, emotional, and uncertain time in Mozambique. We were watching colonial rule disintegrate before us, like spectators in a theatre with no idea how the next scene would unfold. Our counterinsurgency war against Frelimo in the north was so distant, the fight between the Portuguese military and the PIDE [the Portuguese secret police, also DGS] so pointless. Some military, along with PIDE, were fighting the Portuguese central government. Much of our military were in mutiny; many had retreated into their barracks. Everything seemed chaotic.

In Portugal, at 00:20 on the 25th of April, *Grândola, Vila Morena*, a censored folk song about equality and fraternity, was played on *Radio Renascença*, a catholic station. This signaled the beginning of a coup which was later dubbed the *Revolução dos Cravos*, the Carnation Revolution, as tanks rolled into central Lisbon. The Socialists overthrew the long-standing authoritarian regime, an iron rule first under Salazar, now Marcelo Caetano.

The MFA [Armed Forces Movement], an organization of left-leaning junior military officers connected to the Portuguese communist party, deposed of the *Estado Novo*. They faced little resistance in a bloodless coup. When it was over, there were public demonstrations with delight in Lisbon's streets as civilians stuck carnations in the barrels of soldier's guns. We watched, cautiously jubilant.

A book written by General António de Spínola, *Portugal e o futuro*, argued that Portugal's overseas wars could not be won by military means alone. Hugely influential in swinging public opinion and fomenting anti–war sentiment, he called for political solutions to the conflicts. Portugal had grown weary of holding onto their colonies and fighting three simultaneous, very unpopular, wars in Africa. These had only brought isolation from the international community, embargos, and punitive sanctions with decreasing levels of morale in the Portuguese armed forces. This revolution brought democracy to Portugal. It spelt an end to the repressive police state, but the future of its citizens in the overseas provinces was uncertain. The new junta's immediate aims were a cessation from colonial wars in Portuguese Africa, abolition of the PIDE/DGS, and free elections.

A child watches

Lifting myself over the windowsill to get a better view, I felt my mother's two hands grasp me from behind in case I overstretched over the open window. Watching with childlike fascination, I saw a Portuguese flag waved into the wind as I tried to make out the crowd's chants. I sensed frustration in people's voices—anger mixed with despair.

I also sensed an incredible sadness behind me. Looking back at my mother, I saw her wiping a tear from her eyes. All this moved me; not because I was watching my country, Mozambique collapse, or even understood that it was, but because I saw her tears. Years later, recalling this scene to my mother, she remarked that 'I knew at that moment it was all over'. The whole Portuguese population in Mozambique—European, mixed Afro-Portuguese, and Indo-Mozambican—faced an ominous future. We were watching the sun setting on paradise, a red inferno of uncertainty, and a colonial sun dipping into the darkness.

Our fading paradise

Mozambique in the early 70s, especially in LM [*Lourenço Marques*], was a festive place for Europeans settlers. Anyone who lived in Mozambique remembers LM Radio as vividly as their first kiss. 'We hope this helps you say-ey, have a happy day!' The station's signature tune blared through every transistor radio in English, the airwaves reaching South Africa. '*Mammy-blue*' by Charisma seemed to dominate the charts; Demis Roussos serenaded us into further romance, and Terry Jacks haunted us with '*Seasons in the Sun*'. That song was eerily prophetic.

We had the best seafood and barbequed chicken in the world. Residents of LM were called '*Laurentinas*' after the beer, similar to the way people in Rio are called '*Cariocas*'. Even the name had a jolly resonance about it. Three hundred and thirty thousand tourists visited Mozambique in 1973—mostly South Africans and Rhodesians [Zimbabwe]. We called South Africans on holiday '*Bifas*' which would be equivalent of calling someone a 'beef'. Whether it was because they preferred meat when the best seafood cuisine was available, or just looked beefy, I am unsure.

Here we were, hair bleached blond from sea and sun, we were dark and they looked like fair-skinned tourists from Europe by comparison. South Africans loved visiting Mozambique. I too loved my country, spending the long summer breaks in Chinde with my grandparents. This is where the Zambezi River, one of the least spoilt rivers in Africa breaks into the sea in an area full of woodlands, forests, and savannahs. As a child I travelled the region in awe, enthralled by its naked wildness. In Chinde, a black boy around my age taught me how to hunt birds. By early evening, my grandmother had a whole household of servants looking for me.

Mozambique gave me a happy childhood. My country was liberated compared to Salazar's Portugal where Coca-Cola was banned, as well as mini-skirts and pop music. But we children weren't really aware of that.

Scars

Mozambique left me with scars—physical ones. Many folks I meet for the first time always inquire about the conspicuous scar above my eye. It's been there since I was four-year-old and it'll be there for as long as I live. My mother instructed a childminder to hold my hand at all times, as I was notorious for wandering. In a playground, watching kids play on swings, I ventured into one. That's all I remember. I woke up in hospital hours later being stitched for the giant gash that opened above my eye.

By the age of eight, I had come close to dying a few times. I nearly drowned after being caught in a rip current on XaiXai's beaches. Pushed out to sea, I faced a whirling of water, like an eddy, before it sucked me into its vortex. It looked like someone had lifted a plug at the bottom of the ocean as it whirled me round and round. My father, who had rushed to save me, was caught in it as well. I still have flash images of him hanging suspended in mid-water, about two meters from the surface. Those would have been our last seconds on earth. There was a circular sensation just as the lights went out. I came to on a concrete table coughing up water, surrounded by medics. I don't know who pulled us out.

Another close call was nearly falling overboard on a ship travelling from LM to Chinde. My mother skipped two heartbeats as other passengers pulled me back just in time. There is a noticeable pattern, in all black and white photos in the family album; my mother's hands seemed glued to mine.

I even made the front page of the national newspaper. A huge photo that caught the spirit of Lourenço Marques in 1971 saw me carrying a balloon, walking with my mother in downtown LM. My mother is clasping my hand. But then again, the photo was taken as we crossed a busy street, so she had to.

Five days of conflict

The rallies in Estádio Salazar, the stadium in Machava, were menacing from the start. Running for three days in support of Frelimo, they stretched the tension in the capital to a palpable tautness. Power being handed to Frelimo in the Lusaka accords was considered a betrayal by Portuguese in Mozambique. It was one minority rule replacing another.

Adding to the vexation, Portugal's leaders ignored political groups in Mozambique that insisted on being represented in the talks. With the ink not yet dry on the agreement, a group of ex-Portuguese officers from the *Movimento Moçambique Livre*, MML, occupied the Rádio Clube de Moçambique and the airport. Radio broadcasts appealed for support of Portuguese Mozambicans to resist the handover of power interspersed with shouts of, '*Viva Moçambique Livre!*' Long live free Mozambique!

This attempt at a Rhodesia-style UDI [Unilateral Declaration of Independence] gained momentum, hooters blew incessantly and little Portuguese flags waved along every city street. A human wall of support around the national radio station continued to grow. Then it became unruly; a mob of dissenters broke into a prison in Polana, freeing over two hundred PIDE along with other political prisoners.

In downtown LM, a car full of buoyant white students waving Frelimo banners was turned over onto its roof. Students still inside, were rescued by policemen before the crowd's anger could be vented. Then the mood turned ugly; the MML were armed, angry and were threatening to take over the city. Portuguese soldiers watched on.

Samora Machel, fearing MML would start a counter revolution where Frelimo had no operational presence—which was most of the country—threatened to resume the bush war if the revolt wasn't quelled. A group called *Dragões da Morte*, the dragons of death, pushed the tension to near breaking point by shooting indiscriminately at blacks in the *Cidade do Caniço*, the reed city. The black suburbs.

Then came a backlash, mobs of black rioters marched on the concrete city with machetes and sticks. Rumors of a 'black wave' coming to kill whites spread. The killing started in Malhangalene. A friend that lived near the Bairro dos Touros witnessed property and businesses destroyed and ransacked. Dozens of parked cars were set alight.

Portuguese soldiers, still under orders not to use force, looked on. My friend saw a soldier decapitated with a machete; his head kicked excitedly into the dust like a football. Another one had his stomach ripped open as he begged for help in the chaos. Whites were burned in their houses and cars. Corpses were left on the street. The roving mob marched onto Alto Mae before it was stopped by joint Police and Portuguese military.

On the road to the airport, and the one heading out of LM towards the border, vehicles were stoned and set alight. White people were dragged from their cars and beaten to death. Passing convoys of Portuguese going towards the airport shot at black rioters coming from the Bairros. All flights to and from LM were stopped and telecommunications were cut off, but finally, more soldiers arrived with the Portuguese high commission. The white rebellion, not well organized or led, had failed to gain the sympathy or support it had expected from the military.

By the end of the week, on the 13th of September, the first Frelimo soldiers arrived. Most of them were in fact Tanzanians. Frelimo didn't have enough personnel for the task, and these 'terrorists' walking amongst us further darkened the mood. The FPLM [Frelimo/liberation forces] along with the Portuguese armed forces cooperating together formed a transitional government. It was over for us.

Mass, or engineered exodus?

The first sentence in every conversation seemed to be '*ficas ou vais-te embora*?' Are you staying or leaving? An exodus had already started with '*o Sete de Setembro*'—Portuguese were fleeing the country en masse. In fact, the flight had already started in mid-1973 by those that could see the political clouds gathering. A taste of things to come, what Frelimo would later call '*o inimigo interno*'—the internal enemy—caught up with us.

Someone warned that because of my father's involvement in the September revolt, he was under surveillance. To prevent further violence, the Portuguese government confiscated all weapons from their citizens. Like other ex-officers, my father never handed in his weapons when discharged from the military, and was jailed briefly. After the revolt he faced another arrest.

The rebellion exploded again. On the 21st of October, over fifty whites were killed, creating another mass flight into neighboring South Africa. The casualties of both uprisings were around 600 to 2000 deaths, both black and white—estimates vary.

My parents had seen enough. We headed for South Africa on tourist visas. The country had not yet warmed to accepting an exodus of fleeing Portuguese, nor was refugee status being granted yet. We drove out of Mozambique with all our life's possessions in two cars. It amounted to our clothes, bedding, some cutlery, and just enough money to see us through the first month in South Africa. All that represented our family's life's work, including my father's properties, were abandoned.

After entering South Africa, Mozambique was seldom mentioned amongst us. The biggest loss was our close, extended family that stayed behind; it felt like an abrupt amputation of a big part of our lives. Silently, we switched off Mozambique like a light switch.

Our Portuguese government did not have a coherent plan during the transition to independence. Instead, they rushed to scuttle their colonies. There were no guarantees of personal safety for its citizens, property rights, jobs, or pensions. Neither was there protection for Portuguese combatants who had fought in the war; this included thirty thousand black soldiers who'd fought for the Portuguese in Mozambique.

Half of all Portuguese security forces in the African wars were indigenous blacks. In Guinea-Bissau, seven and a half thousand were publicly executed by the incoming PAIGC. The biggest factor for the exodus was the incoming communist ideology of Frelimo, something most Portuguese didn't agree with. Notwithstanding that, no opposition parties would be tolerated in this new society.

Throw them to the sharks

Frelimo didn't represent most indigenous Mozambicans; they didn't win a war against the Portuguese, but were given the keys of victory. Many refugees, now outside the country, held nothing but contempt for the Portuguese government. Mario Soares, the previously exiled leader of the socialist party, became the foreign minister who negotiated the handing over of power in the colonies. He, along with Alvaro Cunhal—the hardline leader of the communist party—had met Soviet officials in Paris in 1973; the political objectives coming from that meeting were now starting to manifest.

The Soviets had offered financial support for the over-throw of the Caetano government, and for the handover of all the colonies. Our collective destiny had been decided by someone else back then. When asked by a reporter in 1973 what would happen to the whites in Africa, he replied '*Atirem esses brancos aos tubarões*', throw these whites to the sharks. Mozambican Portuguese describe Soare's concessions as '*com mão beijada*', a Portuguese expression of kissing a lady's hand, giving something and expecting nothing in return. He became Prime Minister and later President of Portugal.

General Spinola had only advocated for a federal Lusita-nian community with a referendum in each territory on the issue of independence. The MFA and Soares had betrayed us by overplaying their hand; they wanted no referenda.

By 1975, Portugal had almost tilted far left. A failed military coup d'état against the post-Carnation Revolution junta by paratroopers sympathetic to the far left, failed. They were easily repelled by commandos loyal to the government. The political tensions within the MFA, along with a polarization within Portuguese society continued into the 1980s. The US Secretary of State, Henry Kissinger, had warned Portugal of isolation from NATO—an organization itself established to counter the Soviet threat—if it became communist. Some believe that the US was content to see Mozambican and Angolan refugees return to Portugal. They were mostly conservative, their presence and voting base counterbalanced a possible communist takeover.

During the time of the 25th of April coup, Portugal was fighting in three simultaneous theatres of operations. Guinea-Bissau, a small West African country one officer referred to as a 'muddy swamp' had bogged down the Portuguese military, turning it into their Vietnam. In Angola, the Portuguese had all but won the war against all three liberation movements. In Mozambique, the counterinsurgency war had reached an impasse, the seven to ten thousand Frelimo insurgents operated largely from outside its borders. The Portuguese military, kept busy with search and destroy operations, were taking unacceptable losses. Landmines accounted for seventy percent of Portuguese casualties, and ninety-nine percent of the downward spiral in morale.

Portugal's overseas wars took up forty percent of its national budget, yet the psychological damage of young men returning to Portugal in coffins was a higher cost. In the end, it wasn't so much about giving up the colonies, but on the 'how' Portugal did it. When we applied for visas to South Africa, a family friend that worked in a government department warned us that Portugal wanted its citizens stateless. Rumor was they didn't want the pending crisis of returning masses to be their problem. 'Throw them to the sharks' was not just some snide remark, it turns out. Yet, not all Portuguese forces, besides the servicemen, wanted to cease fighting—the paratroopers, commandos, marines, paramilitary forces, and other militia were all willing to continue. The Portuguese were divided about their future.

Similar scenarios were playing out in Portugal's other African territories; five hundred thousand refugees were stranded in Angola. After dragging their feet, the Portuguese government started a *'ponte aérea'*, an air bridge between the 17th of June and the 3rd of November 1975. Shipping and airline queues were up to four months long, many convoyed south in hundreds of vehicles towards South West Africa [Namibia], a protectorate of South Africa. The government was not welcoming of Portuguese speaking hordes of mainly Catholics into their Calvinist state. Many that made it to the safety of South West Africa arrived without passports, were placed in refugee camps and shipped to Portugal. They had faced hundreds of kilometers of harrowing travel through military roadblocks where the three liberations factions were still fighting each other. Countless stories of harassment, robbery, murder, and mass rapes, along the route emerged from this ordeal. A large amount arrived with only the clothes on their backs, dejected, humiliated and traumatized.

A South African national serviceman I spoke to recalled seeing 'ten-kilometer queues' at Oshihkango; many of them were mixed race, which was a guarantee they'd be sent back to Portugal. "Yet they must have been the poorest of the lot," he mentioned in the same breath. About 800 000 *'retornados'*—returnees, a term which was itself a pejorative used to deride their own countrymen—arrived in Portugal. They faced high unemployment, social and political tensions. These 'returnees' were in fact not returning; most had been born in the colonies. Many of them arrived penniless.

The shock of losing everything caused many to suffer strokes and heart attacks before they'd left Africa, others after they arrived in Portugal. There are accounts of people throwing themselves out of windows from high apartment blocks, unable to cope with this forsaking of the only life they had known. This all left a deep impression on us.

With all the skills fleeing Mozambique, an economic collapse was inevitable. The climate Samora Machel created made it impossible for us to stay. Before we left, there were rumors of the *'cercada do Frelimo'*, the encircling of Frelimo that would stop fleeing refugees from destroying everything. It never happened, and although some poured concrete down building drainpipes, drove cars into the sea, and destroyed machinery, they were isolated incidents. These were later exaggerated and portrayed as evidence of economic sabotage.

Mozambique's rapid descent into a pathological ideology

The transitional government suppressed all opposition; any dissent towards the new regime led to imprisonment. A mandatory eight-year sentence was given to 'anyone sabotaging the decolonization process', without a trial or appeal. Reinforcing their Marxist colors, the MFA handed over many Portuguese military personnel—as well and anyone else suspected of involvement in *'o Sete de Setembro'*—to Frelimo, who sent them to re-education camps.

In true Stalinist style, Frelimo's atheist doctrine viewed religion as the only organized force capable of mobilizing, uniting, and opposing the party. A murderous campaign began against Christianity, details which would only emerge years later. In Marxist thought, the proletariat cannot be governed by God, or religion. For the state to be almighty there can be no rival moral authority; right and wrong is decided by the party. Any form of religious instruction was banned in schools, and preaching was restricted. Many church leaders were killed, imprisoned or sent to re-education camps, missionaries were expelled, and church property was nationalized. Frelimo controlled the media and all information coming out of Mozambique. A US diplomatic cable from July 1975 informed this about Machel:

COMMENT: AS IN PAST SPEECHES, MACHEL'S PROTESTATIONS THAT FRELIMO POLICIES AND OBJECTIVES ARE NON-RACIST WERE NOT CONVINCING. TO MANY WHITES. MA-CHEL'S SPEAKING TECHNIQUE IS TO PLAY HYPOTHETICAL ROLE BEFORE AUDIENCE AND ROLE MOST FREQUENTLY PLAYED IS THAT OF WHITE PORTUGUESE OPPRESSOR AND EXPLOITER. HIS REFERENCES TO WHITES WERE REGULARLY TRANSLATED AS "MULUNGO", PREJORATIVE RONGA NAME FOR WHITE. EVIDENCE SUGGESTS, THERE-FORE, THAT MACHEL HAS INTENSE HATRED FOR PORTUGUESE, IF NOT ALL WHITES, AND THAT HE WOULD JUST AS SOON SEE THEM ALL GO EVEN IF MOZAMBIQUE'S DEVELOP-MENT IS SET BACK. PERHAPS BECAUSE OF HIS OWN HUMILIATION BY THE CATHOLIC CHURCH AND MEDICAL PROFESSION, HIS SUDDEN SHARP ACTIONS AGAINST THESE GROUPS HAVE FLAVOR OF PERSONAL VEN-DETTA. RESULT WILL BE FURTHER LOSS TO MOZAMBIQUE OF BADLY NEEDED EDUCATED PEOPLE. NUMEROUS MOZAMBICAN-BORN PRTUGUESE, MANY OF WHOM WERE

STRONGLY PRO-FRELIMO UNTIL VERY RE-
CENTLY, HAVE TOLD US THEY ARE PLANNING
TO LEAVE. IF EXODUS CONTINUES, IDEA AND
FACT OF MULTI-RACIAL SOCIETY IN THE
NEW MOZAMBIQUE MAY SOON BECOME A
DEAD LETTER.

The remaining Portuguese were given an ultimatum:
Take Mozambican citizenship, or leave the country within
ninety days. Yet to receive Portuguese citizenship, one
parent had to be born in Portugal which left some stranded
here. By now, Machel's power was becoming absolute; he
made Mozambicans sit through five-hour speeches with his
trademark of one finger pointing towards the sky. Refusal to
attend his rallies, or trying to leave before the President was
finished, led to flogging or imprisonment. Mozambicans
were told that the land belonged to them, but that the state
would control it. Frelimo never explained to common folk
that 'people' in communist-speak means members of the
party—not everybody is 'people'. Private education was
done away with, only Frelimo's curriculum to be taught.
The dark mood in the country is summarized in this US
diplomatic cable from October 1975:

EXILE OR IMPRISONMENT WITHOUT
CHARGE. REAL OR IMAGINED OPPONENTS OF
"THE REVOLUTIONARY PROCESS IN
COURSE" HAVE BEEN SUMMARILY PNG'S OR
JAILED, USUALLY WITHOUT CHARGES.
MOZAMBICANS OF ALL HUES ARE CAREFUL
WHAT THEY SAY IN PUBLIC. ANYONE CAN BE
DENOUNCED AT REGULAR MEETINGS OF
DG'S, OR EVEN BY SOMEONE HAILING A
FRELIMO SOLDIER.

Private legal practice was abolished, followed by private doctors and medicine. All land, then property, residential and commercial, was nationalized. Freedom of movement was restricted; everyone was required to carry a *'guia de marcha'*—a blue travel document for journeying to another city or province. Cities were divided into communal wards; everyone lived under the watchful eye of the *chefe do bairro*. Anyone who manifested a disapproval of Frelimo's policies or whose views were interpreted as averse to the government was sent for questioning to SNASP [*Serviço Segurança Nacional Popular*, National Service of Popular Security] whose job it was to 'suppress all activities hostile to the revolution'.

Machel's face was plastered on every wall and newspaper, even a portrait of him facing the wrong way in an office could get you into trouble. A Mozambican once told me that Machel didn't want people to believe in God, because he thought he was God. Although this was said in jest, it sounded equally serious.

By his own words, Machel would cleanse his folk from the bourgeoisie's decadent sub-culture. Household televisions were abolished, only collective viewing of government approved communist programs were allowed. Corporal punishment, which he had excoriated the Portuguese for, was reintroduced. Anyone could be arrested for wearing jeans, or a short skirt; women over eighteen could not remain single. Single women, prostitutes, drug addicts, and petty criminals were taken off the streets and sent to re-education camps in Frelimo's 'purification' campaigns. Re-education would create a new man without the values of the rotten colonial bourgeoisie Mozambicans had been infected with. Machel called the camps 'laboratories' that would transform this man into one aligned with the ideals of the party.

Thousands of 'internal enemies' were suddenly discovered, dissidents were executed, tortured and imprisoned without trial. The '*denúncio*' became one's 'revolutionary duty' as Machel berated his fellow Mozambicans to denounce the '*inimigo interno*', even if these where members of their own family. Anyone was a candidate for being part of a conspiracy to overthrow the new government.

The non-existent crimes took on a new dimension. Thousands of supposed PIDE agents, '*infiltrados*', fifth-columnists, and '*parasitas contra-revolucionários*', parasitical counter revolutionaries, were imprisoned. US intelligence estimated figures of up to three hundred thousand imprisoned in these camps; the deaths are unknown.

Climate of paranoia

They accepted everyone into the new non-racial Mozambique on condition that the party's revolutionary ideas were embraced, a heavy-handedness that would have dire effects on the country.

My grandparents stayed behind in Mozambique after Independence to work for the Frelimo government. They had both lived there a long time; being rooted to this land as anyone could be, my grandfather had written a few books on Mozambique. They stayed behind because they sympathized with Frelimo and by all accounts I have, he was well liked by them.

A year after independence, things changed. That dreaded '*denúncio*' was everywhere in the paranoid atmosphere of suspicion. The aforementioned political commissar, Guebuza, gained a nickname of 24-20 because he ordered many Portuguese to leave the country. They had twenty-four hours to do it in and could take a maximum of twenty kilograms in their suitcases. These were randomly picked and never given a reason; those who didn't obey, were executed. Around this time, my grandparents packed up for good—for reasons known only to them. By the end of 1976, ninety percent of whites had left, including many *assimilados*, assimilated blacks and *mestiços*.

A friend's family moved to Quelimane in December 1974. A few months after Machel's visit to the area, the governor came to town. At the Campo Ferroviário, three thieves were publicly executed for crimes so ridiculously petty that they could just as well have chosen people arbitrarily. This was more or less what was happening everywhere else in Mozambique. There are many testimonies of ongoing executions—in the thousands—within the first year of Frelimo's rule; these were accounts from Frelimo's own leadership. US intelligence estimates the figure at seventy-five thousand.

History conspired against Mozambique. Frelimo was an amalgamation of four different national movements who didn't share the exact same political ideologies. Things may have turned out differently had Frelimo's original leader, Eduardo Mondlane, a political moderate, survived. Filipe Magaia, Frelimo's original military commander, like Mondlane, did not embrace Marxist-Leninist ideas. Mondlane was a U.S.-educated intellectual who had declined to comment on which political system he would implement after independence. He was a reasonable person, even proposing a power sharing agreement with the Portuguese government, which was refused. Both men were assassinated in 1966 and 1969 respectively, replaced by a more radical leadership.

Who was behind these hits? It's a mystery that endures to this day. What isn't a secret is that neither was pro-Soviet, which was unacceptable to Moscow. There is credible suspicion that Machel may have been behind these political eliminations. The party was beset by factions and expulsions in its short history. Magaia was 'accidently' shot crossing the Rovuma River by Frelimo troops; Machel would later marry Josina, Magaia's lover. A common belief amongst some Mozambicans was that '*Josina morreu de desgosto*', Josina died young, of sadness it seems. A cloud of mist remains around these conspiracies and the assassination of Mondlane is one of Africa's great unsolved mysteries.

Many that fought against the Portuguese were unaware of the shift to Marxist-Leninism within Frelimo. After independence, they saw the old colonizer of Portugal being replaced by a new one in the Soviet Union. The terror that Machel brought with his transformational policies disenfranchised many leaders within the party. They did not agree with this creation of a Soviet satellite state, or being fed Marxist propaganda. Anti-Frelimo broadcasts were already in effect from a medium-wave transmitter at Gwelo, Rhodesia in 1976, and resistance to Frelimo started as early as 1975.

The general understanding of Renamo is that it had no raison d'être other than being against Frelimo. That is, they had no clear political doctrine. This is true for the most part, but not the entire picture. Reading through early interview transcripts of a 1979 radio interview on *Voz de África Livre*, it's clear that Renamo's first President, Andrè Matsangaissa, considered ridding Mozambique of communism his priority, and free elections the second. Mozambicans did not want to live under a tyranny where both people and land were considered property of the state, or when the state controlled all the means of production. That being said, Renamo's combatants were mostly illiterate peasants who understood little of competing political theories, only what affected their lives.

Frelimo refused to acknowledge Renamo as a counter-revolutionary movement, because doing so would have given legitimacy to the rebels. By the late 80s, Afonso Dhlakama, Renamo's new leader, had reduced his objectives not to win a war militarily, but to force Frelimo into negotiations towards a democratically elected government. Frelimo continued to treat Renamo as illegitimate, yet Renamo was only doing to Frelimo what they had done to the Portuguese in the War of Independence—only on a much larger and more destructive scale.

Our tainted past

Portugal did not adapt to the changing world of the 1950s and 60s, and paid the price for resisting decolonization. After World War Two and the subsequent rise of nationalism in Africa, European powers became aware that colonial rule couldn't continue. Although some European governments prepared African states for future self-rule, they also pulled out of their colonies too quickly.

Salazar saw it differently; he viewed the colonies as provinces of Portugal, and encouraged settlement here. There was no preparation for future African rule; instead, he saw a mixed state. The Portuguese prided themselves in racial tolerance, but the excesses, exploitation, and strands of racial supremacy in the colonies left a scar on the Portuguese legacy. Later, we would learn of forced labor laws such as *chibalo*, debt slavery in the cotton fields, as well as bad treatment of indigenous folk. We would also hear of atrocities by FAP [Portuguese Armed Forces]. Everybody knew of PIDE's torture of political prisoners and the way they eliminated opponents of the regime. That past was soon forgotten as all-night queues for rations became the norm in the new Mozambique. Frelimo was exchanging food for a large arsenal of conventional weapons and hardware from the Soviet Union. Ships full of food, riding low on the water, were seen leaving Beira while his own people starved to death.

The only relevant quote I have from my grandfather was shared with me by a cousin that stayed behind for a few years after independence. The saying is in Portuguese, which loses some of its flavor in translation, 'Where your liberty starts, there ends your neighbor's'. When I asked him what our grandfather meant, he looked back at me slightly puzzled. It would take me a while to comprehend.

A luta continua, the struggle continues

Machel's dream of a non-tribal, non-racial, socialist Mozambique where 'o novo homen', a new man, would be created was a failure. A new man without tradition, superstition, or religion never emerged; what emerged was Renamo. The political ideology that liberated Mozambique was the very basis for discontentment which created the platform for a civil war. The attempt by Frelimo at dismantling tribal structures and their traditional authority was a failure. Their disastrous 'socialization of the country-side' policy bred the very social base from which Renamo could operate. The large-scale forced 'villagization', or communal villages, created a deep hatred for Frelimo which facilitated Renamo's support base.

Many traditional chiefs—respected within their communities—that challenged Machel were sent to re-education camps, or executed. Frelimo's program tried to destroy their cultural heritages, religious practices, land ownership, livestock ownership, and the age-old practice of trading with a resettlement program. Frelimo would justifiably blame Rhodesian, and later South African military support of Renamo, for the conflict. But they have yet to acknowledge that it was Frelimo's laboratories for the 'transformation of man' that stitched together something similar to Dr. Victor Frankenstein's monster, Renamo.

Part II

'I lost so many friends' Vera

10 – Bounce

The transition from trucking to corporate world wasn't easy. A friend found me a temporary job at an IT company in Johannesburg that specialized in Data Communications. Wearing clean clothes and being well-groomed every day brought a fresh feel to this new experience, but it took a while to adjust to the routine.

Our first task was making up computer fly-leads by stripping cables, and crimping RJ-45 jacks at the ends, a monotony that clocked up my first week. Before long, I was missing the freedom of the open road and the thrill of unpredictability, working here was like being on detention. There was some consolation to all this; it was the beginning of a career, even if I was starting it from the bottom-most rung of the corporate ladder.

My first impression of the corporate world was that it lacked a soul. Yes, folk here were very polite and professional, but the whole vibe seemed robotic. In my other world, the tingling of excitement and heightened emotions were normal, but office life was a natural Valium. On my first day, I interrupted a woman for some information, and when a pasty, glazed face with bloodshot eyes turned towards me, that image was instantly welded into my memory. I watched desk-bound workers typing away like slaves, wondering if they needed superpowers to stare at a screen for that long.

Hardly anyone spoke, only the clickety-click tac-tac of fingers running over noisy 90s snap-spring keyboards could be heard. Every few moments the regular 'thoonk' of hitting the spacebar drummed into this hypnotic rhythm.

Within a few weeks, I was splicing fiber optical cables and working on data equipment—the job gradually become more interesting. Whatever my ambitions, in the company management's view my friend and I were only temps, and that wasn't going to change soon. Yah, I wasn't on the bottom-most rung of the corporate ladder; I wasn't even on the ladder yet. The new adventure didn't pay too well, either. I was earning roughly a third of what I had earned in trucking.

After two months, armed with great reports from both my line managers, I approached the firm's owners. I requested a permanent position and was stalled again on a commitment. I'd arrived here with long hair, which may have given my employers a certain impression. The permanent scar over my right eye may have added to the mystique, and perhaps an unwanted ruggedness. What could I say, ditto on that first impressions thingamajig?

One evening, the owner of a nightclub at the 'Wayside' watched me brawl in the street. The club was part of a hotel at the end of Jules Street in Malvern, on the Eastern side of Johannesburg. Some of us called it 'the sideways'. Sideways had also become a pejorative cum adjective for the way some heavy drinkers walked out of the place. It was a typical hotel with 1960s architecture, dull and uninspiring, now one of the roughest joints in the city. Some guys from the '*fietas*', a poor white suburb on the other side of town near Mayfair came to our turf looking for trouble. I was chatting to a girl on the stairs of the entrance when I noticed two friends having an altercation with this group. One was instantly knocked out, lying 'sideways' on the pavement. I had to even things out with these *brekers*.

After the fighting, while trudging up the stairs, the owner of the nightclub, who'd been watching the whole melee struck up a conversation. He asked if I wanted work as a doorman, or a bouncer, on weekends. The rates, along with the perks were good, so I took the job. Security work was not something I relished in, or had given much thought to, but it paid more than the IT job.

On Friday evenings at 20h00, I would start the first shift at the club. It ended when we got rid of the last deadbeats at around 6h00 the next morning. On Saturday evening, I'd do it all again. This was a tough end of town with people getting hurt here all the time.

We were four bouncers; Dannie was a champion boxer, not as famous as his brother Mikey, also a professional boxer. He was better known in the press for his ties to the Johannesburg underworld many years later. There was also Piet who had been the WBA cruiserweight world champion in 1984. I only saw him fight once; more patient, and more of a counterpuncher than Dannie who was a bit slap-happy. In our vernacular, this meant hitting before the unruly patron had explained himself. Another regular was Nicky, who rode with the Hell's angels, a huge guy. You wouldn't want to cross any of them; they were all hard men. I often felt out of place here.

Being alert for so long was mentally taxing. We were targets of reprisals in this testosterone-heavy atmosphere. If drawn into a fight, we had to watch for bystanders with their liberty punches or broken bottles. You had to finish fights quickly to limit the exposure of getting caught yourself. The sight of bloodied bodies being dragged outside triggered the worst reactions in some.

The main door to the club was a thick, solid metal gate with the slit at eye level with bullet pockmarks from drive-by shootings. Let's just say that some people took it quite personally after getting kicked out of the club. Women posed just as much of a threat as the men did; some carried concealed firearms which they didn't declare at the door. Many a scorned partner came looking for a cheating husband or boyfriend. It was a mad place.

We didn't want deaths on our watch; it wasn't good for business, but we got them. On the ground floor, there were two separate pubs, each with its own lounge. In the middle was a mini hall where a band used to play. Above us on the first floor was another club that leased space from my boss, they used us as the first layer of security, but also did their own. One evening before the night was in full swing, a man was killed here. Dannie was shot dead in another nightclub years later. The expected lifespan in this highly-charged arena couldn't have been very high.

One night, I witnessed a commotion across the street. A guy was having a fight with his girlfriend, not slapping her like normal sweaty, white-vested wife beaters do. He was going full-fists on her with lefts and rights until she dropped. She got up only to face the same onslaught again; it was cringing to watch. I walked across the road to satisfy a curiosity; this was out of my boundary. By now a small crowd, probably friends of both were trying to break up the fight.

As I approached, a few of bystanders held me back, thinking I'd come to fight. Seeing me, this maniac, still psyched from dropping his girlfriend became aggressive and put up his fists. I'd said nothing, threatened no one, and done nothing at this point. He bounced around the human wall like a he was spring loaded, but bopped in too close. Although blocked by his mates, I still caught him with a bitch slap—a flat hand to the head. He dropped. His trailing mob complained and murmured as I walked back to the club.

Arriving home that Monday evening a neighbor that lived in the same apartment complex, a middle-aged woman named Peggy called me over. She explained that two pickups full of guys, or something to that effect, came looking for me. Trying out new ammo on the .45, is not always the answer. This security gig turned out to be more irksome than I had first imagined. Being sober for ten-hour shifts had made me see the world differently. I'd begun to hate this shady world of sleazy one-night stands, drunken slobbery, pathetic behavior, stupid people, and now this juvenile revenge. We'd had nights where rows of ambulances and police vans had stood outside when it became really ugly. Life was simpler on the road, perhaps even less dangerous.

I visited Joe, who'd taken over my old F12 Volvo truck, and was busy loading for Maputo.

"How's it, Joe? How's the *situação*?" I asked. He smiled back, but seemed puzzled at the vernacular. "The *situação*, what the Mozambicans call the war?" I explained.

"Ag, it's the same, the same battle. Hey, I got a new prosthetic, it's a Rolls Royce this thing!" It was just peg leg, a casing around the knee, and an aluminum pole with a big rubber at the bottom. Like a pirate.

"She's comfortable, I tell you. The other leg pinched me all the time. I think the flesh under my knee is hardening, it's more comfortable to walk now. But I had to pay three thousand bucks for this bloody thing!" Joe's mood changed at the talk of money. Nothing had changed.

"How's the road?"

"Ag, everyday it's a new story. A truck got stuck at the border last week with donated food from some foreign aid. They turned him back because he didn't have some hygiene certificate, like they can choose with millions starving in the country. African Bureaucracy at its flipping best, I tell you! No one knew the procedure to get the thing through customs. Ridiculous!" It turns out that our displeasure may have been a bit misplaced. We weren't aware that aid agencies often dumped rotten food, expired medicine, and vaccines into third world countries.

"I've wondered. If this run is such a schlep, why do you keep doing it?" I asked with a measure of sincerity.

"You know, my first trip after I got back on the road... Have I told you this? Now, I'm full of guts, not bravado, but more out of necessity, you know. I loaded flour in Pretoria and Artur helped me to sail the load. So, I hit the Witbank highway. The front wheel blows out, *eish...* This will have to wait until the morning. At first light, I started grafting [working]. Now, I must look for a wheel with a good casing in the trailer. I found one, and I put it in the front, all by myself. Jack up, down, put things under the axle, you know... Before I reached the Ultra City, there was another one on the trailer. Ah..." Joe sighed. "I changed it. Just before Nelspruit, another one. Now, I am f★★★★d—no more spares, no more spare wheels, no more guts, no more power, no more nothing." He sounded more exasperated and lost in his own story as it wore on. I let him have his rant, pretending to pay full attention.

"There was a public phone nearby, about twenty meters from me. I sat there looking at the phone for an hour. But my leg hurt so much. I couldn't, I couldn't…" Joe went on, reliving the agony. "I sat there contemplating whether I'd walk around the fence to the phone, or crawl under the barbed wire to get to it. Now, I'm going to tell Artur to take his truck and stick it up his ass, you know what I mean?" He said, grinning. He paused for a long time, as if he'd forgotten the rest of the story.

"Yah?" I prompted him after an agonizing wait.

"Ja…hum, I crawled to the phone and told Artur to come and take the truck. 'Where are you?' he asks. Then I let him have it, you know? He asks me to explain all this to him nicely. I thought I could do it, but I can't. I'm finished! Then Artur goes, 'Whoa, whoa!' Stay there, I'll fix this. So, I crawled back to the truck. Twenty minutes later, a car stops and there were some *porras* from Nelspruit, friends of his. When I got to their house, they had decked the table; there was food, wine, *catembe* [a mix of red wine and Coca-Cola], everything. Then they feed me this incredible meal, one *catembe* after the other. When we finished, I went back to the truck. The wheels were changed, and everything was fixed. And I got two extra spare wheels. 'How do you feel now?' they asked. *Eish*, now I am full of guts again. So, I hit the road and rock up at the border, there by Mananga, early in the morning. Now, you know how long the long truck queue is there. Hmm, hmm." Joe hummed, shaking his head. "Hmm, hmm! You know, they carried me to the border."

"Who?"

"The other drivers from the hell run. They carried me to the border when they saw me. They didn't want me to walk."

"What, on their shoulders, like the hero sportsman?"

"Ja," Joe replied, grinning. "Hey, even the police. Then you scheme to yourself, maybe this is why we are doing it. You know for that, that... I've always been a sucker for brotherhood, and that feeling that I belong. Something for the goodwill of everybody, and everyone does the same for each other."

Maybe it was that simple, I missed that carefree highway.

I approached Harry Thomas, Timothy's boss, for a job. His operation ran exclusively for Manica, later called Ka-Wena. They transported parcels for Mozambican mineworkers living in South Africa as well as foodstuffs. Harry's other two drivers as well as H, who was also pulling for Manica, were the only South Africans going north of Maputo. On the north-south highway, every South African truck had been ambushed, multiple times.

He gave me the work, but wasn't too pleased that I was using his workshop to weld a bench with retractable legs for weight training. Weights were something I always took with; dumbbells, straight bar, and loose plates kept in plastic crates inside the trailer's toolbox. I had to stay active; trucking can be a bad-health trap of inactivity and poor diets. Although I sometimes played soccer on Maputo's beaches, and I'd found an old gym with rusted equipment there, I still needed the flexibility.

Harry also seemed annoyed when he saw me teaching Timothy proper weight training. "Why Harry?" I would ask. "I'm keeping your drivers in shape and out of mischief." He would reply, "Who do you want to *moer*?" I would reply sheepishly, "No one Harry, no one."

I initially took over absent Joseph's truck before the boss

bought another International. Joseph was taking off sick for long periods of time; we didn't realize he was HIV positive. Harry avoided sending two drivers up north to places like Vilanculos when he could. Instead, he would train-up two tri-axles trailers using a two-axle dolly to link them, and send one truck at a time instead. The longest legal super-link in South Africa is a forty-foot trailer interlinked with a twenty-foot trailer, articulated twice. This is done once from the tractor to the front trailer, and again from the front trailer to the back trailer.

With Harry, it was a tractor articulated with a forty-foot trailer, coupled with a two-axle dolly coupled with another forty-foot trailer. This was not of a legal length in South Africa. We would each take a container to Maputo and link both of them there, then Timothy would take the combination up north. Sometimes, both he and Joseph did this. We kept doing this with spare trailers we rotated in Mozambique. If my previous boss was insane with his overloading, Harry was no less so with the length of the trucks he sent up north. That balance between profit and risk...

11 – Spanner

Timothy's truck was shot up again. I heard about it from H at the Manica warehouses in Wadeville. We chatted and listened to music while our trucks were loaded.

"You must check his bonnet, *broer*, it's full of holes," H remarked, dropping the volume on Rodriguez.

"How is he?"

"Ag, he's all right. A bullet grazed his calves; two bullets came through the side door," H explained, rewinding the cassette in the tape deck. "Hey, it's a *kwaai* number this."

"Where was this?"

"Up north, there by Inharrime, you know where the water is so blue, just over the bridge near the sea. I know that spot well. Hey, it's a hot spot."

"This guy's lucky. Is it getting closer and closer?" I was referring to a previous attack on Tim. He'd been bending down to change a cassette when a couple of shots were fired. Whether through the side or the front, the windscreen, I never asked. One bullet hit the headrest.

"Ja, Timothy told me the story last week in Maputo. You know Timothy, he is so calm telling a story, it makes you feel stupid. He and Joseph came rushing into the ambush—two trucks taken out in the middle of the road. He hits the grass off the road, coming in at speed to avoid them. *Broer*, I tell you, it was a lucky escape; the momentum carried him through that sand. As he passed next to them, they let loose with the AKs. Four bullets hit the engine; one hit the dump pipe on the turbo."

"What pipe?"

"The retard pipe on the turbo. You know, by this time the turbo is red hot. Now the oil, it's boiling, and bursts out and the whole engine catches fire. Lucky for the fire retardant under the bonnet, otherwise that Perspex bonnet was gone. By now he was past the ambush, but it was smoking all over. He put out the fire by throwing sand on it."

"What, in the ambush zone?"

"There, a big distance from them." He said, pointing his hand with an 'over-there' forward motion.

"And Joseph?"

"He caught a few bullets in the container; he was just behind Timothy."

"Yah…" I felt the cab rock from loaders dumping goods on the container.

H continued, "Hey, Broer, if they mark you, they mark you. I was on the beach there by Inhambane loading coconuts to bring back to Maputo. Four kids walked up and asked me if I'm South African. I said yes, and they said 'tomorrow you blew'."

"Yah, and…?"

"Ag, nothing came of it. I was held up at Quissico that night. It was too dangerous to hit the road after the curfew. Anyway, I was drinking at the pub when the military rocks up—the commandos, those red beret guys. They rock up there with half the army. Their officer could speak English so we ramble on getting sloshed on some wine. The troops are checking us out, me drinking with their commander. So,

I donate a few five-liter vats of that cheap red wine I always carry with me in the truck. *Eish broer*, I got those soldiers so buckled, the one guy was hanging on the wheel of the truck."

"What, those ugly Russian things with the heavy wheels?"

"Ja, they had two of those with those ack-ack guns mounted on the back with those four big barrels sticking out. Anyway, they even had a field ambulance and a whole armed convoy. These soldiers are so drunk by now they insist on escorting me to Maxixe there and then. 'Come, come my friend, we looking the *viatura* for you. Come, come my friend,' one kept saying, all *lekker* revved up and sparkling eyes. After much contesting, they still insisted. Hey, you feel safe having the whole *mag* with you."

"A night out with Frelimo, on red, red wine, and then...?" I quipped.

"Hey, I had a mate with me that day; he's into some nature conservation for elephants project. While he's there sitting as we groove away, one of the soldiers trains the ack-ack gun on the truck while we are driving, just for fun. Man, the dude shat himself, so I gave him a hit of my joint just to calm his nerves. Anyway, further on down the road... Now, I had just changed the fuel pipe for the long-range tank—some muck must've got stuck in the fuel line. So, the next thing, the truck breaks down from fuel starvation, the military convoy just f★★★s off, and leaves us behind!" H continued, laughing at his own story "Now, it's a dark night, and we are stuck in the middle of nowhere, and I mean in the middle of nowhere. We can see fires burning in the distance and we don't have a clue if it's Renamo, or who. Now, all I need is a fourteen spanner to bleed the fuel line. A number fourteen is an essential spanner, the same size needed to adjust the brakes. F★★k, now we were really stranded, so we decided to sleep on top of the container thinking maybe it's safer in case we get hit."

H paused. "Hey, we need some cold drinks..." he said, calling over one of the laborer candidates at the gate. He gave him money to get us soft drinks from a street vendor nearby. He continued, "I will tell you...There were these two lovers." H laughed rapturously before he could carry on. "These two lovers come walking by. You know, holding hands and hoom-hooming on each other's lips. They come walking past the truck. Now I need a fourteen spanner. All I have is the socket set which is useless for getting into that gap, so I jump down the truck. Man, I gave them such a *skrik*, they took off like they were possessed," H went on, still chuckling. "A while later, this *toppie*, this black dude arrives in a Ford, and asks us if we need any help. I explain the '*situação*' to him, so he tells us he has no spanners, but that he will come back tomorrow to help us. You know, ja right, we'll never see him again. But as true as daylight, six a clock at dawn he is there with his whole family. Man, such incredible people..."

H paused with a thoughtful look into the distance. "Man, such incredible people... They built a fire. The women made us a plain breakfast with coffee. And he brings a spanner. He must have scoured the countryside, and woken up the neighborhood. Man, I'll never forget. So, anyway, I ask him if I can borrow the spanner in case I have to bleed the truck again. I gave him my address here in Benoni and told him if he is ever in South Africa, he must come by. Now, you know what you're thinking at that moment—you'll never see him again. Two months later, I happened to be at home and I hear a knock on the door. It's the old man. I was surprised, thinking man he must be desperate for the spanner as the first thought."

"Are you serious?"

"Ja…" H coughed after taking a drag of a cigarette. "I asked him, you know, joking. He said no, he just came to see how I was. I tell you, I will never forget that black man."

"Yah, that's…"

"Hey, you meet some incredible people on this run, my *broer*," H interrupted before I could finish my thought.

"Yah."

A worker stood in front of the truck with two thumbs in the air.

"Hey, H, this must mean you can take off or land." I joked.

"No, this means your load is finished." He replied, looking in his rear-view mirror.

It took me over an hour to lay out a set of dusty tarpaulins and safety nets neatly over the cargo; by the time I started tying down the load, I was already filthy. After pulling load straps came the ropes, laid in a crisscross fashion to cover the gaps in between. They had to be tightened by hand with the aid of a loop in the middle of the length, each one pulled down with all my body weight. All of this would need re-tightening two hundred kilometers later, when the load had settled. After more than two hours, I was finished sailing up the load. I washed up with a facecloth and drum of water, constantly squeezing out a dripping line of what resembled black dye. Now, I was ready to put on a clean pair of jeans and T-shirt, but as I sat back to relax, I realized how dog tired I was. I hadn't even begun the trip yet.

Thieves and hijackers patrolled South African highways; our country was becoming more lawless by the year. To avoid theft, we never pulled into laybys to sleep. My only options were resting at a truck stop just past Witbank, or fight against sleep until the border.

Driving into the dead of night, I had to keep shaking myself awake, but I'd passed the point of no return. Two mountain passes later, I arrived in the Lowveld, driving on autopilot. Coming up on a secondary road near Tonga, for no apparent reason, I had an impulse to slow down, an instinct that came to me at times. Then I saw the brute; my headlights picked up the shape of a cow sitting in the middle of the road. The tarmac was still warm from the day's sun, cattle often sat here. I crashed through the gears, shuddering through the braking, but the beast just stared at my lights. Coming to a screeching halt, the bull bar poked her hide and she got up reluctantly.

About forty kilometers or so from Border Gate, or Mananga, South Africa's border post with Swaziland, I pulled over into a layby. My head felt like it was spinning. Wanting relax for a few minutes, I was reluctant to rush anywhere. All of a sudden, there were noises of a truck clattering viciously though the gears, and a very loud Jakes ambushing the dead of night. Bright lights shone into the dust storm it created as it stopped, and seconds later, Timothy was at my door.

"I saw your truck pass by Ultra City. I've been chasing you since. I bought us some supper!" He went and fetched a small cooler box from his cab. We sat outside under the stars, my ass on the cab wheel's rim.

"I know you like cheese and ham," He smiled.

"Thanks. I was actually quite hungry." I looked inside

the cooler box. There were fruit juices, cold meats, sliced bread, and of course, cheese.

"We missed each other in Jozi."

"I heard you got shot up again."

Before eating our AM supper, we were invaded by another dust storm, and commotion from a noisy Ford Louisville. His Jakes brake thundered as he downshifted, another one…

"Now my cheese sandwich is full of dust!"

"*Hoesit,* gents?" We were greeted by David Mapena, a colored guy from Cape Town. He was the funniest, most gregarious trucker on the hell run. A well-built young guy who I reckon was the smoothest talker anywhere—the only person I've ever met that can make a black woman blush. He wasn't known for quiet entrances; a man with an undeniable presence.

"Welcome to the 'trucking conference. What's been happening while I was away?" I asked.

"Hello, David," Timothy greeted between chomps on his sandwich.

"Did you hear what happened with the *toordoctor* [Witchdoctor or traditional healer]? Man, chaos… carnage and slaughter!" David went on, unable to hide his enthusiasm and over-emphasizing the 'sir-law-tah' bit.

"Who got taken out?" I asked.

"There was some *toordoctor* at the Namaacha entrance. He was throwing bones around, charging people to predict if the road is safe, you know, by reading the bones. So, people are putting money into the sack and he says the road is clear today. About two hours later, a few trucks were hit!"

"Anyone we know?" I asked. This sounded typical; impoverished Mozambicans invented new ways to hustle money every day. It wasn't a stretch assuming that Doctor Future here had never graduated from any credible bone throwing society.

"No, it was mostly locals. The first was a small, three-ton truck full of passengers on the back. It had crashed into the back of a container. The truck in front had also stopped suddenly to avoid hitting the truck in front of that one. When I came past, it was laying on its side. People were scattered all over—mostly dead; some had been ridden over by trucks coming in afterwards. They hadn't managed to stop in time with all the firing going on. Some of the survivors, as well as drivers were hiding in the bush. One of them wasn't so lucky; after being shot he was placed back into his truck and set alight with it," he went on, unable to tone down a high-pitched excitement in his voice. It was almost a shriek.

"So, everybody rushed into the confusion?" I asked.

"Ag, man, its laughable! When I arrived at the control post in Boane all the soldiers were drunk on cheap wine which one of the passing motorists had donated. Back at Namaacha, the only military vehicle responding to the attack broke down. Man, it was a sir-law-tah, I tell you!" I listened carefully to a slightly calmer David, all the while thinking 'Oh s**t! That must have been H donating that red wine.' He was the soldiers' red wine Santa Claus. I said nothing.

"Why did everybody go in at the same time?"

"Well, you know how people are; the *toor* says it is safe, so everybody storms the road. You know I also had a close call; a bullet grazed my upper back and seat, leaving only a flesh wound." He lifted his shirt to show us the scar. "But the Ford got riddled with bullet holes. I was f*****g lucky, it hadn't been my day to die. There just after the mountain pass, they were firing from the bushes."

"Ja, I heard about that," Timothy said.

"Hey, *bra*, now listen to this! I rock up in Maputo and park the truck there at customs. The passenger I had given a lift to is sitting frozen in his seat, probably still in shock. So now, *bra*, I pull out a bullet lodged in the door handle with the long-nosed pliers. I show it to him, and he faints!" David cackled with laughter. Suddenly, and without taking a breath he changed course.

"So, *bra* Tim, *hoesit* you these days? I hear you are taking plenty of heat from the bandits."

"Ja, the road is getting jumpy," Timothy replied. David, still animated from his own rapid-fire stories, jumped to the next one before we'd finished digesting the first one.

"Hey, the other day... There just before the control post at Boane, I was helping this other *bra* with a broken prop shaft, so we turn it loose. Anyway, I'm walking across the road with this shaft on my shoulder when I hear a car coming, so I turn towards him. Next thing, this car is hammering brakes and doing a vicious hand brake turn. *Eish*, I stood there, wondering what he was up to; he must have thought I had a bazooka lined up on him!" David cackled, slapping his knee before going off on a laughing fit. Tim and I looked toward each other; we weren't sure which was most amusing, the story or the one telling it.

With Tim way too calm when telling us blood-curdling stories, and David too excited with his, we unwound stories until daybreak.

12 – Smiles

I need to digress to another tragedy, Angola. That country's outcome, its suffering, was similar to Mozambique's with equally heavy casualties. After independence from Portugal in 1975, a civil war ravaged this former colony, too. Being on the periphery of this conflict what I recall vividly is not the destruction, or scenes of war, although I haven't forgotten these. It was a human expression that left an imprint on my mind.

The Portuguese departure from Africa in 1975 worried both white minority regimes of Rhodesia and South Africa. Facing a communist onslaught through Soviet expansion on its borders, South Africa gave UNITA military support. The rebels fought the MPLA government, FAPLA, for the next two-and-a-half decades. I was in South East Angola in 1984, not too far from Jamba, UNITA's base of operations.

After a stint with the South African Defense Force's infantry at 8SAI, I was transferred to a special branch of military intelligence, DST [Department Special Tasks], a part of CSI [Chief of Staff Intelligence]. Our directive was to train UNITA soldiers, veterans, and new recruits made up of anything from very mature to much younger men alike. Among all the UNITA folk I'd met, the one most striking in memory is Lusitano. A lighter skinned black man nearing his mid-fifties, he had an air of sophistication, greying white hair, and a very long white beard. He was a driver. I first saw him stepping off a Samil 6x6 truck; during the colonial days he'd been a chef in a restaurant, which didn't explain the swagger. The best way to describe him was a cool dude whom my colleagues called Lucy.

Apart from being a likeable, confident, and well-educated person, it was his mannerisms I remember most. The Portuguese word for s**t is '*merda*', but he used a more polite '*marmelada*'—marmalade instead as in '*esta marmelada*', this marmalade. Ironically, the name 'Lusitano' is a derivative of Lusitania, the Roman name of Portugal. Jonas Savimbi, UNITA's charismatic leader hated the Portuguese, yet the guy's name was literally Portugal. I couldn't help remembering things like this, probably for what they privately symbolized. Yet, it's the contrast between Lucy and another recruit I met that's so profound. The other soldier doesn't have an endearing name, or even just a name, or personality for that matter.

Angola's largest ethnic tribe, the Ovimbundu, made up UNITA's main social base, but they could have come from anywhere. One late evening, a convoy of open trucks came in from the 'interior', bringing new recruits to bases we had in South East Angola along the Cuando River. We were asked to assist with some logistics and getting them kitted out. The images of the next two days became embedded in memory, like photos flashing through the hallways of my mind.

Click. They came sauntering with weary eyes, looking shyly downward. They were barefoot, wearing rags, or a single piece of clothing, over-worn and dirty. It had grown into the shape of their undernourished bodies. To me, the sight resembled rows of slaves waiting their destiny in a previous century. Many of them were just boys; the first kids I'd seen in the UNITA ranks. Conscription would bring them temporary salvation from the miseries of war; not joining meant being caught in the conflict's crossfire. If you didn't choose a side, a side would choose you, or abduct you.

Click. There were rows of black shapes stretching into the bush, yet walking near them, I didn't sense a human presence. They looked neglected and resigned. Pain-hardened faces were incapable of showing emotions, I thought. It was a dark night when they arrived; that may explain it.

Click. They received a green uniform the next day, folded in a plastic with its size printed in a huge letter. Under distant trees, I saw a recruit more fascinated with the plastic than with the clothes. None of them knew what size boots they wore. They had to trade with each other until they had the right size. There wasn't even whispering in the ranks. I wondered if any could speak at all. When they received their webbing and water bottles at last, I saw an expression. Some looked puzzled.

Click. The first meal they received was unforgettable— the way the bowl of porridge was gulped down! Their protruding eyes went white, their faces pulled out of shape as they devoured the food. One kid, after eating, kept running his index finger around the empty metal bowl, scraping up the last molecules. There was no evidence food had ever been in that bowl.

Click. They lined up to receive their AKs, the soldier's symbol of power. I handed a kid no older than twelve an assault rifle with brown grease paper still wrapped around it. He stretched out his tiny hands to receive it, and then he smiled. I may as well have been staring at death's grin; child soldiers whose Kalashnikovs were taller than they were would probably not live long. Outside of the fearful, confused looks, the sole emotion I'd seen on any of their faces was that smile. The expression of that nameless soldier whose face I cannot remember is impossible to forget.

It was a cold happiness. UNITA's revolutionary slogans were almost identical to those of MPLA. It made them believe in their invincibility, the enemy's evil, while being taught to think in slogans and clichés. FAPLA also used child soldiers although the extent is less known, and my reality is only what I'd seen.

But still, it looked comical; the oversized, floppy green bush hats covered their eyes and their tiny fingers could barely clutch the rifle. There was nothing amusing about it, many were brainwashed, their identity replaced by that of a killer. They were cut off from family and cultural environments; now just instruments of war. They, along with the rest of Angola, became a forgotten tragedy. A nation, made up of illiterate peasantry, was plunged into fratricide and conflict over political ideologies they would never really comprehend.

Here in Mozambique, I knew of abductions—the recruitment of child soldiers into both Frelimo and Renamo. Whether for socio-economic reasons, or being lured by lies such as free college education by Frelimo, many a child in Mozambique was trained for combat. The numbers within Renamo were much higher, and here they were taught to cruelly commit atrocities as standard practice. Children were easily manipulated, especially those growing up under superstition and animism. Traditional healers, the 'curandei-ros', made child soldiers think they were invisible; that bullets couldn't penetrate them.

There's nothing like a little sorcery and witchcraft to add intrigue to a conflict, and the unleashing of dark, uncontrollable forces. War's moral lines are already blurry, yet, in a child's mind right and wrong are flexible concepts, making them ruthless and loyal fighters. As for the government, unwilling Frelimo conscripts were often press-ganged into 'serviço militar obrigatório'—compulsory military service. Neither Frelimo nor Renamo admitted to using child soldiers after demobilization, the numbers are hard to quantify; but even harder to gauge, was the lasting trauma and psychological damage.

Timothy and I were near FRIGO, a bonded warehouse just outside Maputo, waiting for some paperwork from an agent. We watched native kids kick about a *bola de catxu*, or *xingufu*, a soccer ball made of rags, rubbers, and plastics. It could be kicked barefoot, but you needed leather feet.

They were jovial, these youth, their excitement transcending the stifling humidity under a hot sun. I would casually join the game for a few kicks and then go back to the truck. This was a dusty, uneven sand patch, chasing a ball with walking boots was clumsy. Crouching low, I placed my hands on my knees, trying to regain my breath. I watched them kicking up another dust storm in a tussle for the ball. My mouth had a sharp dryness, muffling a shout for the ball as they continued clamoring and screaming in the game's dialect. This simple game of soccer had momentarily erased the torments of Africa below the breadline.

In this ambience, thinking about children and war was easy. It was further helped by the uncanny similarity of both conflicts, and a weird familiarity about these kids. Around me, zinc shacks, straw-huts, and a few stalls that never seemed to have anything to sell appeared then disappeared through the dust. Some natives passed by, gave a short glance, and carried on walking. Spectators gazed impassively from the sidelines.

A woman passed near us, carrying a large parcel on her head. A dusty kid was gifted the ball as it popped out of a forest of legs. He dribbled past another one, only to lose the ball in the distance. He was steered further and further away from the field by a defender on his optimistic and glorious attempt to beat the field all by himself. This was followed by a comical volley of scowling and complaints for not having passed the ball to his teammates. One kid gestured passion-ately with both hands with an over seriousness that made it look humorous.

"*Passa a bola, Boer,*" Pass the ball, Boer. I trapped a loose ball with my foot. As my teammate made a blinding run towards the goal, I passed the ball through the dust storm, onto his stride.

"*Fora de jogo! Fora de jogo!*" Offside! Offside! The protests ensued. Racing towards the goal, he made an elaborate body-swerving strike, the ball bouncing off the goalkeeper's legs before uprooting one of the sticks. He came running past in celebration, performing Mozambique's version of the Makossa dance in front of the *fora de jogo* protesters. Reaching out his hand for a congratulatory high-five, I grinned in amusement.

"*Boa!*" Well done! A smile beamed through his dusty face—a grin as wide as the goal line was now a permanent feature. A cynical image flashed through my mind. Trucks could face a Kalashnikov-wielding eleven-year-old with the same enthusiasm, the same gusto, the same grin as scoring a goal. Because out there in the bush, right and wrong, what they celebrate, was mixed up. As my thoughts strayed, another irony wasn't lost on me—the military unit I'd served in, the one had that once trained UNITA, was the same one that had once trained Renamo in Phalaborwa, South Africa. Half a dozen other nuances came at me as I paused, trying to clear my thoughts.

Timothy and I called it a day, leaving the beautiful game to the energetic. We headed towards our trucks and drove a short distance to the Manica warehouses. We sat watching the afternoon drift into a sunset. Workers were offloading flour in one of our containers as we discussed the road.

"Gary and H," Timothy went on, "They hit an ambush going towards Maxixe. It was bad. The first truck, hit by that bazooka thing, spattered all over the place. Next eight, maybe ten trucks, got shot up."

"When?"

"Last week. They ran into the bush with all the drivers. There were about forty vehicles behind that. They burnt the first five trucks, but left H and Gary's truck because they carry containers." Gary was another colleague that now worked for Harry.

He continued, "The bandits take what they can carry and burn the rest. The drivers had to wait about four hours for the fires to die down before they could go again. They had to watch the trucks burn slowly from the bush. It was horrible. They had to push burnt out trucks out of the way with their bull bars because they were blocking the road. Then they had to drive over ashes and corpses, heads popping as they drove over the bodies. There was no time to drag them away; the spot was still hot."

"Couldn't they drive off the road?"

"Sand. You will get stuck."

"How far was H from the ambush?"

"He must have been about two hundred meters."

I asked H about this incident later. The hit was between Xinavane and Palmeira; H and Gary left long after the convoy's departure. At first, they thought it was grass burning ahead, but soon realized that it was *majonjons,* 4–10-ton trucks, in the front of the convoy that were burning. When I asked why they drove over dead bodies, he only said 'the heat'. When trucks burnt, the temperature was extremely high; they couldn't get near them to remove bodies. The other risk was driving near the flames with two thousand liters of diesel in the long-range tanks. 'The heat was so intense, they must have used phosphor grenades because those things burnt until the gearbox,' he told me. His parting comment was, 'This wasn't a war, it was a massacre. Those scenes are engraved in your brain.' The part Timothy mentioned about pushing trucks out of the way with the bull bar must have been later.

"Horrible. Did you ever see any kids attack these convoys?" I asked. Before Timothy replied, there were annoying 'bzz, bzz', sounds of mosquitoes declaring war. 'Bzz', hearing a ringing around my ears I waited, 'slap!' I caught one with a flat hand as it rested on the polished dashboard. Timothy looked at me curiously.

"Got mozzie repellant?" I looked back at him.

"No, I need to buy."

A light breeze blew through the windows, bringing us some relief from the humidity, and those small parasites that carried malaria. Small, yes, but they were Africa's biggest killer.

"*Acabou!*" It's finished. I heard a shout. A knock on the passenger door interrupted us; it was a laborer. At first, he startled me; a black man standing covered in snow. At second glance, I realized that the man had been offloading a load of flour from inside the hot containers, the cause of much sticky perspiration. He must have carried a few leaking bags, because it looked as though he'd rolled in the stuff. All I saw was a pair of eyes beneath the whiteness and black lips move in this pillar of flour.

"The abominable snowman says they're finished," I joked, turning to Timothy.

"Who?" He gave me a puzzled look.

"The snowman outside, the man covered in flour. He says they have finished offloading."

Timothy would take two container loads up to Maxixe the next morning. It was five hundred kilometers of ambush terrain, yet, many beautiful beaches along the way. The accumulative load could reach eighty tons of cargo, but the terrain was mostly flat. Still, this thing resembled a train more than a truck. As we prepared to hook up the combination load, he reversed the second trailer onto the thick metal hook of the dolly as I guided him.

"Come, come... That way, come..." Then a massive click came as the arm hooked. I slung up the trailer's landing legs while a shirtless Timothy assisted by connecting the air pipes. He had a ripped, well-defined upper body.

"I feel good after all this work. Let's go train."

"Yah, ok." I removed the weights out of our tool box-es. We headed towards the workshops of the warehouse complex to prepare our gym.

The training bench was nothing more than a concrete slab with a towel thrown over it. Our area was a dimly lit corner with little space to move around, but it served its purpose. We had to negotiate a slippery floor, and endure the smell of diesel and oil. The mobile crane used for lifting engines and gearboxes was our pull-up bar.

"Tim, I must give you some new weights. These are badly rusted."

"I've had them since Zambia."

"How did you train before you had weights?"

"Bull bar, changing wheels."

"Come, one more rep. I heard the other drivers say you train every morning." I urged Tim on as I spotted him on the bench.

Laborers watched these two crazy truck drivers from a distance. But then they asked to borrow our weights; in return, they'd pack them away. We sat down to rest, drinking water from an old two-liter, plastic Coca Cola bottle.

"Tim, take those two 10kg dumbbells. You can keep them."

"Ah, thank you." He once said—perhaps as light brag—that he'd gotten away with a lot in Zambia at roadblocks. He would show off his big torso under an open shirt to intimidate them. Maybe that was true, but he needed to work a bit more on those shoulders.

The next morning, at the crack of dawn, his truck was idling, building up the air pressure on the compressors.

"When are you coming back?"

"I will be back in a week, I think. One of these days, it will be your turn."

"No, thanks. I don't want to be a slower target. Is there a return load?"

"Yes, coconuts. Sometimes I bring back people," he said as he opened the door. "Extra cash for me." He fired up the Cummins engine.

I smiled, "Coconuts and people?"

13 – Interview

Around August 1992, on my way out of Maputo, I made a routine phone call to Harry. He mentioned a reporter from Johannesburg hitching a ride with Timothy into Mozambique. It sounded like he was doing an article or documentary of some sort on the hell run.

Rolling towards the Namaacha border, I wondered if he was crazy enough to accompany Tim up north. This chap sounded different; some foreign media never left the luxury of the Polana or Cardoso hotels on their assignments. Yet they wrote books and articles about the conflict. I was hoping to catch them in Swaziland, or before they crossed the border, for an interview.

A popular South African magazine, *Scope*, did a piece on African truckers called 'Road Warriors' in January 1989, covering the Zambia and Congo runs. In the interview they quoted Lynne, H's girlfriend at the time, as saying, "When you go trucking, you go with God and tire levers." From what I recall, it portrayed truckers as macho men who lived on coffee and bread. Underscoring the report was that trucking was Africa's lifeblood; without it, the continent would grind to a halt. Besides this ghastly conflict, along with all its nuances, that landscape wasn't much different here. And if I were to do a mock interview on trucking, some meandering was inevitable.

I started trucking because wherever I'd find myself, I wanted to be somewhere else. Feeling the road moving beneath my feet, or just the thought of going to unseen places, soothed the wanderlust. After getting my driver's license and public driving permit, the only work I could find was short term contracting, as a temporary replacement driver.

Around 1988, South Africa was undergoing regular, politically driven, industrial strikes that threatened to cripple the country's economy. We took over absent driver's trucks to the chagrin of the unions; I've had a few bricks thrown at my windscreen, and lived under the constant threat of sabotage. In the growing social unrest against apartheid, trucks burning in the townships were a common sight, and defiance to industrial action was sometimes met with ugly reprisals.

Once, driving one of Mobil Oil's tankers with thirty thousand litters of paraffin to a candle factory, every passing car flashed lights at me on the N12 highway, near Daveyton. A thick roll of wire tied around the back axle was scraping the tarmac, causing a line of sparks to spray out the back. Adding to this coincidence, the dust caps of the fuel outlet valves were deliberately loosened before I'd left the yard. This allowed for a small but steady flow of dripping fuel. If I hadn't stopped, there may have been a fire, or an explosion.

From the start of my short trucking career, driving rigs had always been a fire hazard; this Mozambique gig wasn't a big change in psyche. But still, the image of vehicles aflame always unnerved me; a childhood friend was burnt alive in his car. Coming back from some late-night clubbing, Mario the Greek lost control of his BMW and smashed into a tree. Trapped inside the vehicle when it caught fire, his passengers had to watch him scream in pain as his flesh burnt. "Get me out of here! Get me out of here!"

The entire scene still makes me shiver. I'm not sure which is the most chilling; the sight of burning flesh, or the horror-stricken screams. In English, we use the word 'inferno' for a fire that's out of control; the Portuguese use same word for hell. It's everyone's worst horror.

David—not David Mapena—of JH Transport had just passed Boane when he came across one of those scenes that are impossible to forget. A large bus had been hit by a rocket, an RPG or bazooka, and had been incinerated. The skeletal wreck was blocking the road, which meant he had to squeeze alongside it, passing rows of seats at eye level. "Those people were charcoal," he said.

On a different note, Africa long-haul has unique characteristics and undesirable distinctions. Truckers often told me of partying for days, but within the same breath mentioned waiting weeks to cross borders. Rushes of excitement and absolute boredom are parallel lanes on this road, along with all the carnal temptations.

Smuggling is one of the biggest incentives in cross-border trucking; everyone has done it, even if in small or insignificant amounts. Some wealthy entrepreneurs who own fleets of trucks and properties in foreign countries made their start with contraband. There are many secretive, remote locations, accessed after hours of cruel roads that are used to load, or offload illicit goods. As for commodities like minerals, most of the Congo and Zambian truckers I'd come across had smuggled them, especially cobalt.

A friend was approached in Zambia with an offer of eight uncut diamonds. After testing and confirming their value, he purchased them for $4,000. Everything went fine until leaving the country; he was searched by the authorities and locked up. The penalty was confiscation of the stones and a $4,500 fine. A few months later, another trucker approached the same friend for some advice on the authenticity of eight diamonds he wanted to buy for $4,000. My friend warned him of the swindle, but he didn't listen and suffered the same fate.

As long as there is greed, there be will con jobs. In Africa, you shouldn't stray from the business with which you are familiar. Wherever there's a profit to be made, the police, or someone high up, may not be far from the deal. In Mozambique, there was a saying that you're safer with criminals than with police; it's the same in much of Africa. Then again, I also know of multi-millionaires that made their initial fortunes from diamond deals—it's a mixed bag of prizes.

Never give passengers you don't know a ride across borders, especially women. A trucker, Jan, previously with us on the hell run, was given a seven-year sentence for smuggling drugs while taking a load across Botswana. The woman riding with him left a bag of mandrax under the seat and disappeared during the search. He died after two years; Botswana's prisons are harsh.

These things can happen so quick. H, too, was locked up in Lusaka Central prison, Zambia, for two months on a bogus charge. In his words, he 'almost lost his feet', having to stand crouched on a wet floor for days on end. Yet, in the same conversation he also mentioned once breaking down near a village in Zambia, and having two of the best weeks of his life. The chains on machinery he was transporting for the mines, broke; he couldn't move the truck until they were replaced. Stopping a passing truck, he gave the driver a phone number to contact for help while he jammed his music and made new friends for that duration.

"I met the most incredible people in that place," he told me, without elaborating. As a white man, you learn that unless you make friends in these countries, and embrace African cultures, you will be a lonelier man for it. But don't get too involved either, not everyone who drinks a beer with you is a friend.

Joe was approached in Angola when it opened trading with South Africa after their civil war. They asked him to bring in a super link (two trailers) filled with maize with payment to be made in diamonds. Jokingly, he asked where he was supposed to get a truck full of maize from. The Angolan merchant look confused, "You hijack the truck and bring it here, of course."

Looks could deceive; the sight of a driver with an aging truck, struggling to make a living, wasn't always what it seemed. I'd seen large trucking operations crash, deals going bad, and loads not paid for. Sometimes, it was because drivers ran away with trucks loaded with expensive goods into countries like Tanzania.

Shady deals were more costly than the price you'd think you'd pay; they took you further than you wanted to go, violated your conscience, and stole your peace. You couldn't ask God to protect your truck on the corridor of death while carrying unlawful goods; that'd be shameless and delusional. To survive this gig, you'd have to shun temptations. Many truckers had died in custody, usually from malaria. Opportunities, risks, and dangers lurked everywhere.

FAM's ineptitude in dealing with rebel insurgencies, along with banditry, was the cause of ninety percent of casualties. They were incapable of mobilizing an effective counter-offensive against Renamo, and the conflict had reached a stalemate. Notwithstanding that Mozambique was by now a humanitarian disaster. The increased presence of Zimbabwean and Tanzanian troops with Soviet gunships in the countryside had further alienated the peasantry who disliked Frelimo. Concentrated raids on villages and Renamo bases by the ZNA, the Zimbabwean National Army, from the mid-1980s onwards, left more devastation. Aided by Frelimo's ongoing destruction and burning of villages, especially in Zambezia and Tete provinces, by 1992, about two million people had fled the country, mostly into neighboring Malawi.

Proper studies, reports, and the real extent of Mozambique's calamity would only emerge after the war. No thanks to Mozambican journalism that seemed ideologically bound in upholding the Marxist revolution, sanitizing the horror by withholding facts. Missionaries that reported Frelimo's scorched earth tactics; massacres, and destruction of villages were branded as Renamo spies, or as right-wing propaganda. Frelimo's control and manipulation of information wasn't bullet proof though; many of their atrocities would eventually be exposed. In the meantime, people in Maputo seemed to have a better grasp of International matters than events in their own backyard. Still, a certain naivety persisted; some dear souls still believed that their mainstream media reported news without bias or governmental censorship. Then again, the revolution had survived longer than it should have, because of deliberate ignorance.

Even food was weaponized. Frelimo controlled all donor food, having previously withheld aid to all that refused resettlement. As Frelimo emptied the fields of peasant farmers, agricultural output declined in the communal villages, which in turn made the country dependent on western agencies. However, donor food could destroy local agricultural economies still in operation by creating an oversupply—stock like maize cost less on the black market than it did to grow it. Western donors were rewarding Frelimo's failed policies, and much of the food disappeared into local markets before it reached crisis areas.

Roupas de calamidade, good quality used clothing, meant to be handed out to the less fortunate was, and still is, being sold in markets today. Water filtration kits donated by the EU, earmarked for specific projects were being sold in Maputo's informal markets. Frelimo refused to let aid into peasant areas where Renamo was known to operate from, but according to other reports, it was Renamo refusing access. Starvation had become the real *situação.*

Closer to us, violence came and went in cycles—sporadic at first, then more regular. You could hear distant gunfire on the Namaacha-Maputo stretch; at other times it was near Boane at night, and often on the outskirts of Maputo, or sometimes inside Maputo. Either the army barracks at Boane were being revved by Renamo or it was just FAM firing at ghosts to shake out their fears—a miniature version of the countrywide saga. If there was excessive gunfire on the corridor, soldiers at the checkpoint wouldn't let you through. Trucks had stood up to three days at Namaacha waiting for things to calm down before being allowed to continue.

As far as we were concerned, Frelimo was no match for Renamo. A few kilometers from the Boane barracks as the road lifted on a hillock next to a quarry, there was a light blue container on the side of the road. The area behind this landmark was a temporary base used by FAM, lined with trenches. Soldiers would be offloaded here by truck at 7:00 AM, and picked up in the late afternoon. One morning, Renamo were waiting for them in the bush. As they were being dropped off, the rebels opened fire, cutting down [probably] around twenty soldiers. Even if they had taken up their positions, it may not have made much of a difference to vehicles. A South African trucker whose name I can say but can't spell was being fired upon from the side of the road in this area. There was large dip nearby with massive holes in it; trucks would come to a near standstill negotiating the uphill. We kept deviating further and further away from the road because it kept deteriorating. That section had become a massive hot spot. After fleeing his truck—which he left idling—he ran into the bush, and landed up the trenches with them. He implored the frightened troops to fire back at Renamo. They didn't.

Even the animals suffered; Maputo's zoo could not feed its animals due to the scarcity of food. Isaac Scott, another transporter, once took three truckloads of half-starved animals back to South Africa free of charge. Charity, a willingness to help, and integrity—many truckers refused to carry an iota of illegitimate cargo—were also in abundance here. The last lions of an Egyptian bloodline were taken to Tzaneen. God only knows the utter devastation of animal life in this war, not to mention Gorongosa National Park where huge swaths of wildlife were killed.

Particularly galling was the apathy of government officials. Recently, two South African trucks had been shot up just outside Namaacha. It took the trucking bosses a long time to repatriate one of the drivers' bodies. The corpse was released only after much bribery and argument; that, after being left neglected on a table, and badly decomposed. This same ritual was performed with other corpses needing retrieval; you'd think by now they would have a better system. Fortunately, they allowed the wounded being sped off towards South Africa instant access across the border. It was only the dead that had to wait.

Somewhere between Boane and Namaacha, in the middle of the corridor, I saw a familiar white, International S-Line. Those two chrome exhaust pipes sticking out the sides of the cab were unmistakable. We stopped a few meters from each other's bull bars as I alighted from the truck. I greeted Timothy, then shook hands with the reporter, a young white guy who looked to be in his twenties. "Was he doing interviews?" I asked. He looked bewildered.

"Um, okay," he replied, scanning the surrounding bush anxiously. In my lost-in-thought-ness and enthusiasm I'd forgotten where we were, but I couldn't back out now. He fetched his tape recorder and fiddled with the microphone's cable as he walked back towards us. Playing the cassette backwards and forwards, he found the spot from which to record.

"Tell me about the truckers on this run." He held up the microphone towards me, the sounds of two rumbling Cummins engines idling in the background.

"Most truckers believe in God."

"That's good. Can you elaborate on that?"

"No," I replied. He quickly snapped a photo of Tim and me posing in front of his truck.

I've never seen him, that picture, or the documentary ever since. It may have come out in the Scope magazine in late 1992. It's the only one taken of me on the hell run that I'm aware of, and the only interview I've ever done, in person.

14 – Matches

H's most recent habit when telling a story was to pause after the climax, then sign off with "Incredible!" Now he'd adopted the Portuguese 'incrível', and the more emphatic 'incrível pá!'

"*Incrível pá!*" He said after a pause, laying it really thick in the middle of *in-creee-velle*.

"Then he grabs the money and says thank you!" He was recounting the previous night's episode, when a policeman approached him as he climbed into his truck in downtown Maputo. After some squabbling and the usual remonstrations, he was ordered to go to the *esquadra*. Using his saltiest language, he told the cop to take a hike. He 'fired up the Oshy' and pulled away, only for the man to jump on the steps of the cab and grab the rear-view mirror frame.

"It's pelting with rain, my *broer*. This cop must have been smoking some good stuff. I'm picking up speed and he's hanging on, commanding me to stop. Now the rain is crashing, you know—it's like drums on the roof of the cab. He's getting pelted, giving these synchronized blinks of the eyes…" H went on, laughing heartily. "But he just hangs on! Then he pulls out a pistol; it must have been a point two-two, or a 7.65 caliber, and he shoots at the front wheel!"

"What, at an angle?"

"*Ja*, and he jolts the gun as if bullets will come out faster. So, after three shots he gives up and bangs on the window with the butt of the pistol. I ram the brakes, hard. He goes flying towards a puddle of water doing ballerina skips and arms swinging. So, I open the window, holding out some money for him. Hey, I was thinking this guy was going to be really *bedonnerd*, but he walked up and took it."

"What, no further argument?"

"*É pá*! I don't know what he was looking for, maybe on the fornication patrol." H tee-heed. "*Eish*! He must have fallen off the happy tree that night." H smirked and after the regular pause, a silence wafted into the cab.

I gazed over the seaport at the edge of the Manica warehouses in Matola. I enjoyed a moment of calm, thinking about this cartoonish event. Vera once remarked, sniggering, that some of these [crazy] things could only ever happen in Mozambique.

"*Incrível pá*!" H muttered to himself after nearly a minute of silence, shaking his head in disbelief.

It was also Vera who clarified the detail of the incident. The police had spotted her getting into a vehicle with foreign number plates and went after her for prostitution. Mozambican nationals were prohibited by law from doing so, which wasn't the case here, because Vera was a Portuguese citizen. H didn't understand the argument in Portuguese, got irritated, and took off. After the wild rain drive, she flashed her residency card and scolded him. The cop apologized, but H still hadn't figured out what the commotion was about, and threw money at the problem when he didn't have to. I still prefer his version of the story, though.

An incredible blues number came on as H clicked his

fingers in harmony with the song. He pulled out his *bak*, his guitar, from the bed, and tried to play along.

"*Eish, eish*," H whooped to himself as the music on the stereo shifted into an incredible blues chord. His stringing-along work sounded more like plink-plonk noises in the background.

"Who's this?" I asked.

"Hey, *broer*, I don't know, but its incredible stuff. A Malawian driver gave it to me in Beira. I never saw him again."

"There's just one problem." He turned down the volume. "It's driving me crazy!" he joked, laughing heartily.

"What? It's good stuff!"

"*Ja, broer*, but the cassette is stuck, it won't come out." He clicked the eject button furiously. "I've been listening to it for a week." We both laughed.

"On serious note… if you're running to Xai-Xai, how's the road?"

"You must take matches with you," he chuckled "Hey! Have I told you this story?

"What story?"

"The one about the matches?"

Yes or no didn't matter; he was going to tell me anyway.

★   ★   ★

Just before Marracuene, you are diverted onto a weigh-bridge that hasn't worked since colonial days. Arguing with the officials is futile, but you'll be told that 'the [East] Germans have fixed it'. Once you've negotiated a penalty for overloading, you may continue on your way. From here, you have mostly tar all the way to XaiXai, but the surface is so bad that trucks with a single diff struggle to get through. Burnt-out vehicles have created massive craters, and the road has deteriorated so much that small trucks regularly become stuck.

Just past Marracuene, in Bobole, there's an old, Portuguese canteen on the left side of the road. Its fading walls are pocked with bullet holes, and the doors and windows are missing. This ghostly building marks the spot where the queue for the *coluna*, the convoy, starts. Cordial vendors sell fruit on the broken, concrete stairs. Bands of them have descended, since the two to three-kilometer line of vehicles started forming.

On your right-hand side is a row of *barracas*, wooden stalls that sell the best *Galinha Cafreal* (spicy chicken) in the whole country. The finest last meal you'll ever have. But the *menú diario* will be trucks throwing prop shafts, overheating, and bursting tires on this trip. Anyone not inside a vehicle that's ready to depart is super friendly; you can strike up a conversation with anyone here, as if you'd known them forever.

Mozambique's weather forecast is mostly awesome all year round. It'll be another gloriously sunny day; that's a good outlook because bad things only happen when it's gloomy and overcast, right? The fresh morning smell of the bush and diesel trucks idling has a familiar feel as you wait to advance. After a swig from a warm Coca Cola bottle, you bite onto a mini loaf of dry bread—this is breakfast, all you've space for. To relax you take a drag of a *Palmar* cigarette, a local brand, but it tastes like straw. It's flicked out of the window and picked up by a grateful passerby who smokes it like his life depends on it. Dusty kids in rags with toothy grins stare at you.

Folk music plays softly on the stereo. But it's that Eagle's song '*Witchy woman*' that plays louder in your head. Joe once told me that during their ambush the Eagles were playing full blast. That song played right through the firing until a bullet lodged in the cassette player and the music died. For a brief moment, H tried to switch it off.

"So, the bandits killed witchy woman?" I asked facetiously, but got a puzzled look in return. I asked him again if witchy woman was playing during the ambush. Yeah, he replied, chuckling. I still don't think he got it; maybe his mind was elsewhere.

You perspire in the heat and humidity, waiting for the military escort in front of you to settle. Although the corridor to Namaacha was dangerous, the heat map of the war was north of Maputo, around the Manhiça and Gaza districts. Because of its distance, the government's protection of the corridor was different here. The EN1 national road faces north. FAM drops off a truck full of soldiers every few kilometers in front of the convoy. They're Zimbabweans by the looks of things. In front of you there are funny looking armored cars, BRDMs. There are private vehicles used by the military, green military trucks, BDRs with mounted Russian twin barreled 23mm cannon. There's also a fee for the escort—well, more a donation of cigarettes and food to soldiers; from here onwards there are fees for everything.

Behind are about eighty vehicles; you can't see the tail of the *coluna*. It's filled with cars, mini-buses, makeshift buses and a variety of junk on wheels. Apart from the occasional South African, or foreign truck, there are no semi-trucks to be seen. There's only 'rigids' as we called them—all local trucks, which all look old and patched up. There are Bedfords with dull, primer like paint, and plenty of yellowing-ivory old Mercedes's with round bonnets. All of them are overloaded, have balding tires, and poker-faced people squashed in the back. The most interesting passengers are goats balancing on top of buses that are missing side windows. The most interesting cargo is stacks of empty, blue fifty-liter water drums tied to the sides of buses.

A ten-tonner coming from the other direction whistles past, teetering dangerously to the left, the back-axle's alignment is inches off. You tap your fingers on the steering wheel in impatience.

Everyone heaves forward. The convoy caterpillars along, stretching, driving onto each other's bumpers. There are black fumes of exhaust smoke belching everywhere, people waving as the convoys rumbles past. It's impressionable; the clunkers that will run this gauntlet make you shudder. Within a few minutes, the convoy feels like a slow moving *confusão,* confusion. Too many vehicles clumped together is claustrophobic, if a vehicle breaks down, we all became easier targets.

And break down they do.

The road is narrow; it's tight, bringing everything to a standstill when a vehicle fails. Fellow travelers will try and help you, just to get this whole thing going again. In the rainy season, it's much more fun, especially when the road 'disappears'. You have to point your truck at the mass of water and hope you stay on it. Some rigids will stay in it, some won't.

The convoy clatters along at fifty kilometers per hour; you'll be in XaiXai in four.

They ambushed this initial stretch of road near the town of Taninga on the 31st October 1987 according to AIM reports I've came across. The rebels destroyed eighty vehicles, and killed over two hundred civilians, which they left scattered all over the bush. A month later, further up the road near Maluana, they killed sixty-three and wounded seventy-eight on another attack on a convoy even though it had a military escort.

AIM, the Mozambican news agency reported that thirty-two burning trucks and buses lined the road for almost a mile. The burnt bodies of some drivers were found behind their steering wheels according to the report. One truck bore markings of the U.S. Agency for International Development. The cargo of food, destined for the drought-stricken provinces in the north, had been partially looted before being burned.

Another report from AIM on October 18, 1987 said that the rebels ambushed a convoy of vehicles on the nation's main north-south highway—this same road—and killed at least fifty people. Survivors said another thirty people were wounded. About half of the fifty vehicles in the convoy were trapped in the ambush fifty miles north of the capital of Maputo. Witnesses said they'd been fired at from both sides of the road, the bandits running through the vehicles robbing and gunning down people. Vera remembers the days of these attacks. Radio broadcasts requested volunteers to report to Maputo's central hospital. Trucks were coming in, offloading bodies in piles. "*Corpos, corpos, todos baleados…*" "Bodies, bodies, all full of bullets…," she said pensively.

In the official response to the '87 attacks, Renamo blamed army deserters or counterinsurgency units that wanted to embarrass them. This may raise an eyebrow, even if only slightly. It seems like a missed opportunity; why would the rebels deny the killings if the purpose of their existence was to terrorize Frelimo and the countryside? The internet and other archives I've searched since have little reporting of attacks on convoys in the period of 1991-92. Yet, during this time, they'd take out twenty or more vehicles at a time. The closer we got to the end of the war, the more gruesome it became.

As you progress, you'll see all cover up to eight hundred meters from the road has been cleared. Trees have been cut down, all grass and vegetation has been set ablaze. The black, charred earth will go on until Inharrime, 170 kilometers past Xaixai.

All four attacks that Timothy had faced so far were in the Inharrime region, which could read that the clearing was effective until then. Here and there an empty, bullet-ridden house in the opening will keep you alert while you watch for any sudden movement. But at least there's visibility of the approaching menace. This is where H's dictum of, "If they fire from distance and they fire too early, you brake; if they fire late, you accelerate," came from. He'd been fired upon four times with an RPG, a rocket-propelled grenade. Three of them were in the vicinity of Xinavane, even though Zimbabwean soldiers were normally present there.

In one instance, returning empty towards Maputo, he saw a bandit lining him up with an RPG from the right-hand side of the road. Normally, Renamo wouldn't come in from the left—the side parallel to the sea—to avoid being cornered by the ocean and FAM, or Zimbabwe soldiers. He saw it being fired but couldn't outrun the rocket which struck just below the container. It was resting on wooden railway sleepers, one of his modifications. After a minor blast, which couldn't have been caused by high explosive or anti-tank projectiles, it set the wood alight. As he bolted out of there, the wind fanned the flames which caused some panic. He quickly unhitched the trailer in case the fire spread to the tractor. At the entrance of next town, he stopped an incoming truck to ask if he'd seen his trailer, and if it was still ablaze. No, the fire had blown out.

Among the many, there was a massacre in 1991 that could have been avoided. A shipment of brand-new cars was delivered to the wrong sea port. Whether it was due to sea conditions in the Mozambique Channel or was just an administrative screw-up, we don't know. They were offloaded at Inhambane instead of Maputo. It appears that all these vehicles, mostly Toyotas, were for government use.

Drivers were hired to take them down to Maputo in a convoy. About thirty kilometers from Inhambane, on the EN1 split; all of thirty to forty vehicles were shot up. H and Vera arrived soon afterwards to a macabre sight; the smell of charred bodies and burning rubber still permeated the air. One car, partially scorched, had blood splattered on the new plastic seat cover. Another stretch of Mozambican road became a motor vehicle scrap yard.

The road leading towards Inhambane, in both directions, had become the most dangerous in the country. Not that any in the whole region was much safer.

The railway line between Inhambane and Inharrime as well as the railway line leading out of XaiXai was also attacked. All the south-north roads in the Manhiça district and Gaza province were regularly ambushed. Yet, initial vehicle ambushes on the south-north highway had some honorable conduct. In the beginning, earlier on in the war, Renamo used roadblocks and ordered passengers off their vehicles with their belongings. Cargo was confiscated and taken to temporary bases deep in the bush. When FAM started escorting vehicles and firing back at Renamo things changed, many attacks became massacres.

A *Washington Post* article from January 24, 1988 headlined 'War Pushes Mozambique toward famine, collapse' mentioned this of CARE International, an independent relief agency, "Since 1984, CARE officials said, 15 of its truck drivers and assistants have been killed in ambushes, 75 trucks destroyed or seriously damaged and 450 tons of food and relief supplies looted or destroyed by guerrillas. They said another 500 tons of commodities was stolen, or destroyed in attacks on warehouses." CARE ran the largest food distribution program across Mozambique; continuing after these setbacks is a testimony of human resolve. You could also say that driving through ambush country after being slapped around was the ultimate screw-you to bandits.

Among her personal tragedies, Vera recounted how she lost one of her best friends on this road. Zequinha, someone she'd grown up with, was attacked near Palmeira. His vehicle, a small closed truck, was obliterated. He'd just given ten soldiers a ride. "They shot the truck with a bazooka," she went on, to which I queried how she knew it was a bazooka and not an RPG projectile. "The size of the hole," she said with a solemn look.

A friend from Scott's transport, Frankie, told me of another convoy that was incinerated while standing still. Running past the curfew time, a group of eight to ten trucks didn't want to drive at night, so they pulled over into the sugarcane mill just past the town of Xinavane. The trucks riding behind ignored them, carrying on towards Maputo. This layby cost them, they were all killed that night and all their trucks burned. I may only have scratched the surface of tales this road has to tell.

Niceties ended here. When vehicles break down and can't be repaired you shove them off the road, pushed aside with the truck's bull bars. The road must be free of obstacles. If you were stuck, the more powerful trucks would chain you out of the soft sand, or tow you away from a hot spot. Two hundred and fifty thousand Meticais was the price, the going rate, you'd be told. Slower trucks, the stragglers, with their excessive black exhaust smoke are left behind.

Everywhere seems to be potential ambush terrain. Two tanks appear on the side of the road, one with broken tracks, the other burnt out. You lose count after fifteen broken down Russian T-54s—funny that, all their hatches are missing. They didn't close properly? Removed because of the heat? Near the bridges there's always shot up and burnt-out vehicles. Until Xai-Xai, there will be around a hundred and fifty burnt-out vehicles, mostly pickups and smaller trucks. Many of them are overturned.

At the main bridge over the Limpopo River near XaiXai, there are ten skeletal, rusting vehicles lying on each side of the entrance. This is clearly a hot spot. There are pedestrians and people everywhere to be seen in the small towns. During the curfew hours of 10h00 to 15h00, they all support Frelimo; but once the curfew ends, the eerie silence returns to the bush. Who knows? Some of the people looking at this convoy with interest may be wearing Renamo garb tonight.

More people lived in little plantations and scattered communities along the corridors than anywhere else in Mozambique. This corridor, like the road from Beira to Maputo, was not in anyone's control, neither by Renamo, Frelimo, or their Zimbabwean allies. The distances were just too long. It's full of deviations, obstacles and pot holes. Burnt-out vehicles, used as road blocks, mark old hot stops, destroyed houses along the way paint the mood. Yet, for most of the journey, you see no one; it gives you a feeling you're on your own, Jack.

A vehicle is stuck. Soft sand, drying mud and turned-up earth has proved too much for an overloaded rigid truck. The truck had no name; it had no bonnet either. It's probably an East German model. The single file cuts through the bush—not all obstacles deter the flow of traffic. It's not always the thought of an ambush that's daunting; it's the thought of breaking down that causes the stomach to tighten. Did you remember to put chains in the toolbox?

The most striking image is despair on passengers' faces. When a *chapa* (the public transport) breaks down in a dangerous area, everybody wanders outside while they try and repair the vehicle. Driving past all you can do is offer them a thumbs-up; you know that these ageing, rotten trucks have little chance of getting on the move again. Further down the road, you drive past a whole family whose pickup looks like it has a damaged axle. You wave, but your best wishes only reveal a fear in their eyes as you roll past. Being stranded in bandit territory must be utterly unnerving.

There's a peculiarity that catches the eye. On every trip, you will find eight to ten new accidents; vans, pickups, and sedans overturned, many of them government owned. The sheer number of potholes, the inexperience of drivers, a deceptive impulse to speed, slow moving tractors, and farm vehicles that suddenly enter the road are all contributing factors. But judging by the low amount of traffic passing through, it's only a partial explanation. The only certainty, without exception, is that all these vehicles will be stripped bare within a couple of days.

By now, the convoy is dispersed. The sight of many swaying palm trees calms the mind; from Xaixai onwards they're everywhere. Two dropped off Zim soldiers are sitting high on a telephone pole, using it like a crow's nest with a cover over their heads. Is this for show, or an actual OP? They could be targeted; it would take them a while to come down and take cover. Oh wait… there's little of that. These guys are toasting in the sun, their bodies shine from the sweat. They always ask you for water. Further down the road, another group is doing the same OP thing. They have no radios, so what's the point of all this?

In the Manhica province, you might see a few men in civilian clothing with AK-47 rifles guarding something, largely private estates. They are civilian militia, trained by the military, perhaps British DSL, apparently fed and paid by private farmers or enterprises. Small, private armies had become a norm for farms, estates, and factories.

On occasion, larger bands of Renamo rebels attack, and take over a small town in these districts. They'll ransack it for food, clothes and alcohol along with the rape and murder of some civilians. The survivors will flee the town into the nearby fields and await a response from armed militias who will recapture the town with little effort as rebels scatter into the bush. This whole scenario will replay itself weeks or months later.

It was not uncommon to find ex-rebels now used by private militia groups—at least they wouldn't need to feed off violence against the innocent. The *confusão* was that whenever you saw anyone with an assault rifle, you froze. Friend and foe looked the same.

After living on the edge of his nerves for so long, H

started laughing at bandits who were firing from eight hundred meters away, always at the edge of the clearing. "Ok, it was whisky courage," he admitted. "But it's always uncomfortable hearing bullets hitting the container," he would say. The north run was H's story, everybody knew him. I doubt he was ever sober on this run, but sobering it was.

★   ★   ★

"No, what's this about matches?" I quizzed.

"Hey, somewhere between Manhiça and Maçia I hit a contact, coming in at some speed. I drove into the middle of a small-scale battle, happening there on the right side of the road," H said, pointing to the truck's right-hand side. "Small arms fire ratatated away, followed by the thumping of heavy machine guns bursts retaliating aggressively. So now I'm wondering what I've just driven into, and if I'm in someone's kill zone." He continued, shaking his head.

"*Broer... Broer*, next moment this soldier in camos is standing in the middle of the road, ordering me to stop. Now, I've no idea whether he's friendly or not. The way that guy trained that heavy caliber machine gun on me, I could tell that he was determined to make the truck stop. Tires dug into the road, brakes whined and gears crashed through the gearbox. The whole rig vibrates as I slow down. This soldier stares at me with a blank look. 'Me Zimbabwe soldier, officer of this platoon,' he said very hastily. 'Yes?' I asked him, and at this point I just don't know what to think. Now, the heavy firing is still banging away in the distance. 'Have you got a match?' the guy asks me, flicking his hand." H continued, striking an imaginary matchbox.

"*Broer*, now I'm floored. Does he want to light a cigarette in the middle of this war? Now, you know the soldiers on this road are always drunk or high, always asking for ganja or matches. They never have matches. I wasn't even sure if he needed matches to light up a doobie. But then he completely floors me. 'Quick!' He says. 'Renamo have got us trapped. The wind is blowing away from the sea, they are coming from inland. I will set fire to the grass and drive them away.' I threw him a lighter. *Broer*, I was getting more nervous by the second. But I was in such a hurry pulling away from there that I pushed the gear into high range instead of low and broke the gearbox. Well, not all broke. I had two gears to get out of there and that's how I drove all the way back to Maputo. I only had second and ninth gear, I can't tell you what a mission it was, especially on the up hills. Eventually, Timothy caught up and towed me for the majority of the way when we got back into South Africa. At one point, it started to rain heavily, a total downpour, and Timothy just floored it. Timothy was overtaking vehicles, water spraying up so bad that I couldn't see the back of his truck, or his lights. I was being towed by a madman who didn't use brakes. *Broer*, I was more petrified with his towing in the heavy rain than that contact. *Incrível pá!*" H said, with a look of horror, shaking his head.

"*Incrível pá!*" I echoed, after a long pause.

15 – Law

I suspect that when the Portuguese left Mozambique, one of their officials tore out pages from the only copy of the national *Código da Estrada* (road code) just to confuse the Mozambicans. That is said with the tongue firmly in the cheek, yet it's not beyond the realm of possibility.

The only traffic violation that the police seemed to be aware of was *'você pisou na linha'* which means 'you drove over the line', or 'you stepped on the line', which means nothing. We didn't know if the rules allowed us to cross the line when overtaking or moving around an obstacle. We were unclear what line this was referring to—a solid, broken, white, yellow or red line. Most roads in Mozambique were in a very poor condition, few had visible lines or lines at all. Still, *'você pisou na linha'* was our most frequent traffic violation.

I arrived at H and Vera's house in Maputo and was greeted by her at the door. At times, she could be quite chatty, and before long, we were caught up in a spirited conversation.

"Hey, Vera, he's here to visit me," H said gruffly.

We all sat in the lounge, with me drinking tea of all things. The talk drifted into bad police behavior as I recounted an event that happened in Maputo in '91. I had almost unlocked the secret to neutralizing police harassment, don't stop when they tell you to, if they're on foot that is. On normal days, that is, and hope they don't grab the rear-view frame and shoot at the wheels, of course.

I had just arrived with a load from South Africa, trundling down Avenida 24 de Julho, when an angry-looking policeman waved me down. Stopping meant blocking a whole lane on a very busy downtown street; it wasn't as if there was a pull-over lane, so I ignored him. An annoying, aging blue Peugeot 504 slowed the truck by brake checking me on a descending road towards the harbor. The foot policeman had apparently commandeered the next passing car to chase me down. Before getting to the 'you stepped on the line' part of the story, H's eyes lit up with an I-want-tell-you-something look on his face. "That reminds me of something similar that happened to me," H cut into the climax of my story without realizing that I hadn't finished it yet.

"F★★★★g *incrível*! It was literally like Laurel and Hardy, a fat cop and a skinny one." H rattled off another tale "I was coming back from Chokwe, there just past Macia when these two stand in the middle of the road with arms flailing, ordering me to stop. I wasn't going to stop or in a mood to stop. I already had a couple of drinks in me, and I was in a hurry. But f★★k, these guys were determined to make the truck stop. They refused to give way even though I wasn't slowing down. How were they going to catch me if I didn't stop? With what? They had no vehicles!" An animated H went on. He looked at me bright eyed then stared into space and shook his head "One of them still had a glass of beer in his hand!" There was a pause before H collected his thoughts. Then the story's tone and speed changed, like if he was going up through the gears.

"They insist on getting into the truck. For what? I ask them. They want me to chase down a four-ton Mitsubishi that has just driven past and refused to stop. They insist that this four-tonner is stolen. How do they know? 'Just drive,' they say. Now what? As we pull away, the fat cop takes a last sip of beer from his glass, and chucks it out of the window. I floor the rig, trying to catch it. Now, I was coming back empty you know, so I had enough speed. A few kays down the road, I see the small truck. It's a white truck with those tarpaulin covers on the side, like a *chapa*, but it's full of woman and children. Now what? I must push that *chapa* off the road. 'What?' I shout at them. 'Are you mad?' The next moment the cop sitting on the inside of the passenger seat takes out his nine-mil and shoots at the Mitsubishi alongside us. F★★k! If we hit a pothole this drunk p★★s might shoot the other cop in the head!" H grabbed both his hands and cupped them over his face in a display of disbelief as he explained all this to me.

"As we come into a slight uphill, I overtake the four-tonner and cut across the road, forcing him to stop. The cops get out, both of them. I couldn't see what they were doing below the cab. Then I took a gap, I pulled away, the passenger door closing itself as the rig jerked into the road." A pause ensued as H disappeared into his own faraway place of thought.

"And then?" I jerked him out of his silence.

"*Ag*, I blazed out of there. The cops know that drivers transport people, coconuts, and some goods on the way back to make some side money; they just want a cut of the business." There was another pause as I sipped my rooibos tea, but this break was just H getting ready to uncoil another story.

"But that's nothing compared to what happened at Ponto Final!"

"Yeah?" Ponto Final was a private house in suburban Maputo. As with much of Mozambique, many households had '*guardas*', guards with Kalashnikovs, used as private security. Some were recognizable by variants of green uniform, attire that did not guarantee adequate training, or any training at all, I suspect.

"We're sitting at Ponto Final. There's a *casa* [house] there on the corner. Me, another helicopter pilot friend, and a couple of mates from a nature conservation gig are having a party. We're drinking and singing, using the tables as drums. It was a very merry night, banging the tables and playing the guitar. Then the front door crashes open, like a cop raid. In comes the *guarda,* and drops off a dead body on the floor. There was a stunned silence. This is the same *guarda* I paid fifty thousand meticais to look after the Oskhosh outside. 'He was trying to steal your batteries,' the *guarda* says. So, he shot him…in the head!" H threw me a bewildered look "In the head! Can you believe this? In the head!" Then he paused, like he was suddenly reliving his own tale "We paid him another fifty thousand, and told him to go dump the body up the road." He stared at me with wide eyes that were saying '*Incrível*!'"

Perhaps it wasn't that incredible, or even a surprise. Vera had an AK pressed to the head by these building guards, once violently grabbed by the arm. I've heard of them getting drunk and firing at each other.

The story I didn't finish was that after being stopped, I wasn't at all cooperative with the policeman, or his newly deputized Peugeot civilian. We civilians were supposed to work together against the police, not assist them. There was a fracas on the sidewalk and it came close to getting ugly. I happened to know that it was unlawful to transport any government official in a civilian vehicle. Yet, the policeman decided that arresting me was the best course of action, so we drove with him as a passenger in my truck, to the *5ª Esquadra da Polícia* near Polona.

Cuca, my loyal Mozambican friend, came to talk with the station chief to 'correct the situation'. While sitting on a bench outside the office, I overheard the banter between them. The commander, a portly man with a large moustache spoke with a sober tone. "This is a very serious business," he said, at least twice.

At this stage, I was wondering how much time I'd spend in jail, but was more obsessed with not having mosquito repellent to take with into a cell. I wasn't sure if it was a good time to be concerned about my immediate future. Cuca quick-wittedly joked with the police chief. Then the unexpected happened, the chief shot back with a very humorous comment. A policeman with a sense of humor, I found that unnerving, I'm not entirely sure why.

Another option to mitigate the harassment was hoping a female policewoman stopped you. Then you could ambush her with annoying fake questions like 'are you married?' and 'don't you like South Africans?' This fanciful theory was posited by David and H, who both got away with murder using their special edition of Portuguese. This was especially true for David, the boisterous one with a comical adaptation of the language.

I lacked such social skills; my Portuguese was too precise to sound charming. The closest I ever got was an angry policewoman stopping me, her hyena snarl with the dagger stare made it look as if I'd murdered her young. I'd crossed a line.

Not that broken Portuguese was necessarily a good thing, as H discovered. On the runs north he would always be stopped by one particular policeman. Waiting at the entrance of the town of Manhica, about eighty-five kilometers from Maputo, this official would always wave him down. They began to develop a relationship; laughing, joking, and back slapping over small talk every time he passed through. I suspect that there was an element of pretending to understand each other, although and they did speak about music at length. That, everybody understands.

Inevitably, the cop began to ask him to bring small things from South Africa, and if H remembered, he would. One day, he upped the ante and asked him to bring him a *ferro de engomar,* H didn't understand what this was but he knew what *ferro* was, it was iron. *Engomar* is the older Portuguese usage of the more modern term *pasar*, as in to pass with an iron, or ironing clothes. He asked around but no one could clarify the mystery, on his next trip he asked the policeman for a more precise explanation of what he was looking for. He did, by making hand movements with his right hand, doing strokes over an imaginary cloth on his left hand with an iron.

'Aha!' H replied. 'I know exactly what you want!' When he arrived in Johannesburg, he went shopping for this special thing. He had to find a place that specialized in these unique products. On the next run up north, like clockwork, he was waved down by the policeman.

"*Bom dia, senhor H.*" Good day, mister H! The policeman smiled.

"*Howzit?*" H replied, grinning like a Cheshire cat. "Guess what I have for you?" Very proudly, he pulled out a box that had cost him a fortune and asked the cop to open in. He waited in anticipation.

"*O que é isso?*" What is this? He looked puzzled. It was a violin bow.

★   ★   ★

Being more natural with Portuguese had its advantages. Once, after being stopped by a policeman on a 125cc motorcycle near Matola the first thing out of his mouth was, "*Você pisou na linha!*"

The first thing out of mine was, "*Sujei?*" Did I dirty it? I said with a deliberately confused look. The look on his face was worth the fine, which was about ten US dollars, the highest value of any fine in the system.

16 – Peace

Frelimo and Renamo signed the peace accords on the 4th of October 1992, bringing an end to fifteen years of civil war. Finally, the healing could begin, but the conflict had cost a million lives, along with an immeasurable amount in trauma and suffering of these poor people.

A group of South African truckers, on hearing of the treaty, remained in Maputo the following day, a Monday, to celebrate. To us it spelt an end to driving near vehicles aflame, crouching behind the steering wheel whenever you heard gunfire, and having ice run through your veins whenever anyone stepped onto the road. Although a few remained skeptical, most saw this development as an end of the bloodshed. At FRIGO, a group of truckers drank beer and reminisced about war stories, near misses and experiences, the partying and guffawing carried on until the early hours.

The best time to leave Maputo towards Swaziland was at around 8:00 AM, allowing sufficient time for soldiers to take up positions along the road to Namaacha. On Tuesday morning, five drivers left in four trucks, one of them getting a ride to the border to fetch his vehicle. This convoy left earlier than usual, probably at about 7:00 AM, or perhaps even earlier.

Joe left by himself, at around the normal time. Arriving

at Boane, he noticed that there was hardly any traffic; there were few people about and activity was below normal. Was everyone still celebrating? Was it a public holiday? Trucks would normally hang around at this checkpoint, watching for traffic arriving from the other direction. It was a rough indication that the corridor was safe to travel. But being the only vehicle on the road made him feel more alone, something just didn't sit right. An hour went by, and still no soldiers arrived at the boom. The army must be hung-over from some partying, he thought. He fired up the rig and accelerated into the corridor.

Near the turnoff to Goba, just past a small steel bridge, as the road veered left, the there was a row of gum trees on either side of the road. As he approached them, he saw a column of smoke rising ominously. Gripped by an instant fear, he slowed down. Moments later, a row of stationary trucks emerged, partially concealed by the trees. He stopped, looking around anxiously. There was no movement, not a soul in sight. 'I was s*****g myself,' he later told me. 'I didn't know if bandits were still in the area.'

Minutes that felt like seconds passed before he finally ventured towards the convoy, each step feeling heavier than the previous one.

A gruesome sight awaited him; the truck at the back of the convoy, a Ford Louisville with a flat deck trailer, was smoldering. The driver, sitting upright in his seat, was already charred by the flames; his passenger had been tied to one of the wheels and burnt, too. Looking around nervously, he felt only a cold, dumb silence. Scurrying past the second Ford Louisville, Bongol's truck, no one appeared. Reaching the third truck, an International Paystar, he noticed bullet holes in the cab, but also missing a driver. A fair distance ahead stood a Mack truck driven by Daniel from Scott's transport. It was peppered with bullet holes and showered with broken glass, blood everywhere on the driver's side of the cab. There was no sign of him either.

He walked on the shoulder of the road, returning towards the second truck and found a body in the bush just next to the road. There was a small bullet entry in the head and one to the chest, the back of his skull was blown off. This looked like an execution. Joe knew this black driver, Josiah, well; they'd been friends for years. Grabbing the body by its legs, he dragged it towards his truck, but couldn't lift him onto the flat deck trailer. He kept trying and kept failing, feeling as though he was about to have a mental breakdown. Suddenly, a yellow minibus appeared, followed by a hurried explanation with the driver. Passengers immediately got out to helped load and tie Josiah down.

Numbed by the whole spectacle, he drove into a thick silence. Potential danger still lay ahead, but turning back didn't feel any safer. While a gnawing vulnerability pervaded, there still was no sign of soldiers protecting the road. It was a ponderous drive to Namaacha where he arrived, still shaken, to ask the locals for directions to a morgue. He was directed to a place to drop off the corpse. As he approached the boom at the border post, he was mobbed by a dozen people, including other drivers. His was the first truck to arrive this morning, he was told; with uncertainty and unease about travelling, no one ventured into the corridor. Joe's hardest task was to call Veli, also a trucker, to inform him of his brother Josiah's death. He vividly remembers him sobbing like a man in agony over the phone.

As Daniel, riding in the front truck of that beleaguered

convoy turned into the long curve he saw two of them stepping into the road. "I thought they were coming from that village," he said, referring to a nearby settlement.

The firing opened up from around eight hundred meters away.

"They shoot here in front of the truck," he went on, pointing to the floor. It was a familiar modus operandi; firing low into the ground, with searing lead licking up the dust and bringing the line upwards into the target. Just then, another group emerged from the bush and started shooting in rapid fire as well. Facing a hail of bullets, he ducked beneath the dash, behind the truck's long bonnet, but left his right shoulder exposed. Two bullets ripped into him, knocking him back and off the seat. A projectile locked the accelerator into full revs and another burnt a hole through the sole of his shoe. Not far past the ambush, he stalled the truck. Bongol, following behind him, stopped and ran into the bush while the bandits took aim. He was hit on the side of the head, dropped and feigned death. Having to wait until his assailants had vanished back into the bush, he headed towards Josiah's Paystar, which was still idling, and opened the door.

A body fell out of the cab, so he dragged it and placed it on the side of the road. In the meantime, some villagers had arrived and picked Daniel up with a blanket to drag him to safety just as FAM soldiers and a civilian van appeared. Plugging the wound on his shoulder with his own T-shirt, they insisted on taking him back to Maputo for medical help. He refused to go back that way, "If I die, it's going forward, to South Africa," he told them.

When asked to pull out his tongue, and seeing that it was white, his helpers remarked that he wouldn't even make it to the border alive. It was Bongol who convinced them to take him, jumping into the back of the van with Daniel. All the way to Namaacha, he slipped in and out of consciousness before arriving at Brown's filling station.

The owner was also a transporter. Brown fetched a Bible, loaded him in his vehicle, and drove like the blazes via Swaziland and Mananga to Nelspruit. "He prayed for him all the way," Frankie, from the same company, remarked. Daniel survived that ordeal; he still drives trucks today, but with limited movement on his shoulder.

When I asked him how many bandits there were in total, he only said, "Plenty". Jimmy—another trucker friend of ours—remarked that it looked as if they'd drilled holes through the chassis. The dual rails are made of high tensile pressed steel; it may as well have been cardboard, bandits loved using armor piercing rounds. Similar to H and Joe's ambush when Jimmy went to recover Daniel's truck, he counted around eighty bullets holing the cab.

I later asked Joe why he thought this attack happened. He looked at me pensively and blurted, "I think it was them saying f★★k you for signing the peace treaty." An alternative explanation is that the news hadn't reached the bush yet. Joe's flippant assertion might even be the correct one; there were those who didn't want the conflict to end. Many within Frelimo profited from the war, and the government received more International aid because of it. People made a living from it.

Jimmy suggested that white drivers weren't regularly targeted, or killed by Renamo. This goes back to their training by the SADF in the early 80s, and based on a conversation he had with an operative of the time. He was told that Renamo kids were trained like robots, who to kill, what to destroy, and who to spare. There is further support for this idea after an incident in 1990.

Mario, a white Portuguese driver with a Scania 112 gave a FAM officer a ride on the Namaacha-Maputo road. Seeing a group of bandits ahead, eleven to twelve-year-olds (their age may be slightly exaggerated in the way the event was explained to me) the officer ran into the bush, jumping from the moving vehicle. He hid in a ditch as the truck rolled towards a stop. Just as Mario was ordered to climb off the rig, the other bandits found his passenger and executed him on the spot before setting the vehicle on fire. Mario's life was spared, but because he'd given a government soldier a ride, his truck wasn't. The idea of whites being spared because they might be South African may explain Braam's close escape in 1986.

Another not too dissimilar, but equally puzzling event happened in 1985 to Vera's father who was a white Portuguese man. On his way from Maputo to Mbabane, in Swaziland to buy groceries, he ran into a group of heavily-armed combatants on the Namaacha road. They weren't wearing the olive-green uniforms of regular soldiers, but camos. This would usually mean that they were Korean, or British trained Special Forces, but not necessarily so. He waved at the three of them he saw and they waved back, stopping him to ask for cigarettes before letting him proceed with his van. When he reached Mbabane, he phoned his family to inform them he had arrived safely, something he always did. Just then, he heard the news; all hell had broken loose; a line of cars and pickups that hadn't been far behind him were all shot up and set on fire.

The theory may be partially true for the mid- to late 1980's, but doesn't ring true for the 1991-92 period. H and

Joe's ambush is the most obvious example; plenty of white Mozambicans driving smaller trucks and pickups were killed on the corridors. The Namaacha hotel owner's son was also killed on this road, along with people of color in the same car. When Renamo attacked a convoy, they didn't discriminate by skin tone, or spare anyone because of it.

My reluctance to convoy was probably correct; in a group everybody gets hit. If you're alone, they might let you pass and wait for a bigger target. Then again, it wasn't only the rebels ambushing trucks, so those rules wouldn't always apply here; it depended on who was doing the attacking. What adds further credence to the theory is in the 1980s 'Renamo branco', white Renamo [white Portuguese businessmen outside the country] supported the rebels.

Renamo were better organized than I'd first thought. After the war, I learnt of at least one base within the Matutuíne District near Ponta do Ouro, right on the edge on the South African border with Kwazulu-Natal. It came after Jimmy and some of his friends investigated the disappearance of a Portuguese resident from Namaacha. The family was ambushed on the Maputo road, all of them scattering into the bush when Renamo opened fire. Correia and his older son survived, his daughter was found un-harmed in a Catholic convent weeks later, but his other son was held captive by Renamo. He later died from hunger.

Frelimo must have known about this camp, but never attacked it; the perimeter was likely mined. Besides, Renamo were very mobile and would probably have received a tip off. There were Renamo members living within the cities, especially within Namaacha. They spotters, informing them what was on its way. After the war, a Renamo officer boasted to Jimmy that they only needed

MIGUEL A. MITRAS

six members to attack a convoy of any size, and knew exactly what vehicles were on their way. It's a chilling thought – before you left town, you may have been marked for death.

17 – Ban

On the Thursday morning before the treaty, I was parked between two warehouses at the Manica complex, waiting for a signal to move into offloading position. I was lying on the bed, feeling spent and fatigued; I hadn't been sleeping well.

Suddenly, there was a knock on the door, my cue to start up. I jumped behind the steering wheel, but there was no one to be seen. As lay down again, I heard another knock. Getting back behind the driver's seat, I saw a laborer walk away in the distance. A little irked now, I tried to get some rest again.

'Knock, knock'. This was followed by another, and another. I watched a procession of laborers, each taking a turn to knock as they walked by. They were doing this to goad me. It wasn't the first time either; I'd gotten the feeling that they enjoyed provoking South Africans.

About ten paces away their supervisor turned around, glaring at me behind the wheel. That smirk on his face only annoyed me further, and I climbed down.

"*Então?*" I asked seriously, only to be met with dismissive laughter.

"*O que é isto?*" What is this? I demanded as I walked towards him. Any remaining goodwill disappeared when he began speaking loudly over me in Shangaan, his native language. I didn't understand a word of it, only certain he was doing this on purpose.

"*Estás a gozar comigo?*" Are you mocking me? I asked. He said nothing.

A massive quarrel ensued. Mauro, the warehouse manager, wasn't much help in dealing with the problem. I landed up in a heated discussion with the *chefes* who also insisted in speaking Shangaan, even implying that I was being racist. But they had the leverage and after some tit for tat they decided to ban me from entering the premises. As if that wasn't enough, I overheard one say that they'd finish this on the road. I'd had a bellyful of this.

Harry transported exclusively for Manica, meaning that running loads for this company was over. When I phoned to inform him of this 'development' he wasn't moved, saying I could still pull trailers to the border. Then there was that threat about watching my back. All just empty talk, but it still left me with some uneasiness.

I avoided sleeping in the truck that night, booking myself into the Rovuma instead. It was a low budget, but well-kept hotel in front of the large, Roman Catholic Cathedral in downtown Maputo. Just before lying down, I had an urge to vomit, throwing up everything I'd eaten that day. Now, I couldn't fall asleep. There was little else to do except exchange some banter with the barman in the hotel lounge and watch television. The movie was lame, but the subtitles kept me entertained. It was the weak translations from English into Portuguese; specifically, slang used by US combat soldiers that amused me. Without warning, a message came across the screen which said 'Fin de transmissão', end of transmission. It wasn't even a digital image, someone in the television studio was holding up a white paper across the screen.

End of transmission.

"Ai... isto é assim?" So, is this how it is? I asked the friendly-looking face behind the counter wiping a beer glass. He replied that the TVM technician had ended his shift. It's 23h45, the guy decides it's time to clock out, so he goes home with twenty minutes of the film remaining? The barman shrugged his shoulders with a wry smile. I went back to my room and vomited again.

Unable to sleep, I left Maputo at 5h00 AM the next morning, opening the boom myself at the checkpoints. By the time I'd reached South Africa, I was fatigued and had a strong urge to lie down. The rear-view mirror showed that my eyes were yellow. I wanted to put a blanket over my face, and kiss the world goodbye until I felt better, but Harry needed the truck in the yard today. My whole body ached as I rolled lethargically towards Johannesburg. Seeing a doctor upon arrival, I was diagnosed with jaundice; he put me on a restrictive diet and insisted I go home for three weeks and do nothing but rest. At least it wasn't Hepatitis or Malaria. The infection must have been from the local water; I didn't drink alcohol, do drugs, do piercings, tattoos, or sleep around.

I wasn't aware of the peace treaty, or of that Tuesday morning's ambush until it came up in a later conversation. While resting at home, my friend from the IT company came knocking; they wanted me back. There was an upcoming project in Mozambique, installing data communications for the Railways and it would help to have a Portuguese speaker on board. My first reaction was, "You're joking, right?"

On my first day at work I asked my boss, Johan, if he

realized that travelling to Mozambique by road was hazardous.

"Ja, that's Ok. We're flying in." He replied.

★   ★   ★

The attacks on the corridors did not end with the October accords. For the next two years, bivouacked government soldiers still protected the roads from freelance and social banditry. When the Ressano Garcia border was reopened towards the end of 1992, a ghastly sight awaited travelers; the road hadn't been cleaned up since late 1989.

Vera, driving with H on their first trip since the reopening of the border counted over two-hundred and fifty burnt-out cars, trucks and buses on the stretch between Moamba and Ressano Garcia, not counting the dozens of vehicles buried by the terrain. There were trees growing in the middle of the road; nature had reclaimed much of it. As it was on the Namaacha road, drivers were warned not to step off the road which had not yet been de-mined.

"There were huge craters on the road from burnt-out vehicles," she told me. "They [the government] took three months to remove all the vehicles. My body would go cold when driving past, many of them still had skeletons in them, after all these years! Only after three months did the panorama change. I still get shivers when I think about it..." She rubbed her forearm. In one of the vehicles there was a skeleton with an expensive watch dangling from the wrist bone. Nobody tried to remove it due to some superstitious beliefs.

H was more lighthearted about it. Running into some fresh travelers on this stretch, they asked him how long it took to travel the road. It was six hours then, nowadays it's about twenty minutes. He replied that you judged the distance by how many bottles of brandy you had left to drink.

The treaty did not persuade everyone to hand in their weapons; Renamo took over five towns in the country's north which were retaken by FAM afterwards. The demobilization of the two militaries would prove to be a challenge. Some of the military were in mutiny in parts of the country for not receiving wages and over a lack of job opportunities after being discharged. Disabled soldiers demonstrated over low pensions, and newly unemployed veterans threatened a new wave of banditry and looting. Then there was the small problem of actual bandits who made a living from attacking and looting the corridors—attacks Renamo sometimes took the blame for—that needed to find new ways of making a living.

Two months after leaving trucking, I visited H in Wadeville where he was loading. Jumping onto the passenger side of the truck cab, I greeted him, "How's it going?"

"*Hoesit*?" he replied in a hushed tone. During the awkward silence that followed, he seemed lost in thought.

"How's the road?" I tried to restart the conversation that was stuck in first gear. H handed me a photo.

There was an upturned, mangled truck with a steel container that had turned oval. The bonnet was ripped away exposing a familiar engine and an unmistakable shape of a white International cab. Seeing patches of brown, I wasn't sure if it was dried blood or mud. I recognized the container by its distinct, faded blue; this truck was definitely Timothy's.

"Good grief, H! What happened?" I said, rubbing the photo.

"We planted him…"

No one knows what happened. On route to Maxixe, just before the fork to Inhambane there were tracks from an army truck digging across the road. It looked as though they'd cut across Timothy's path. That stretch slanted to the side; to veer off the center was perilous. He may have done that to avoid a collision. Pulling two trailers with forty-foot containers was tricky; if he corrected his line too quickly, he may have caused the trailers whip and snake out. With this configuration, it takes over a second for the weight to transfer from the back to the front, snapping the steering would cause the whole train to flip on its side.

They had looted the load by the time David and H arrived. Everyone knew that FAM also attacked trucks, stole goods, and blamed Renamo—this looked suspicious. A government unable to feed its soldiers is crime waiting to happen.

Timothy was unrecognizable; at first, they couldn't confirm it was him before noticing the cowhide Zulu band on his wrist. H told me that the two 10kg dumbbells I'd given him had crushed his legs.

Friends collected Timothy's belongings while waiting for recovery vehicles to arrive. When H opened Tim's wallet, he closed it again, it was as if he didn't want the photo of his wife and son to see the horror. When the corpse arrived at the morgue in Maputo, it was left unattended outside in a casket, decomposed and swelling in the heat. David arrived here soon after. With emotions still running high, he perceived this as neglect and lost it. He dropped one attendant with a punch then went ballistic before being restrained. Sometimes, you felt like doing that in Mozambique.

Colonialism, lives, friends, even television transmission—Mozambique had become a story of early endings for me.

18 – Ironicles

After seven years in the Information Technology, I left the last company to start my own business, first as a contractor and later as a consultant. The work dried up, so I took a sabbatical. The plan was to immigrate to Europe due to the IT and Telecoms skills demand, but I delayed the process for as long as possible.

After doing an open water scuba course in Sodwana, on the North Coast, I decided not to return home, staying on the beach for the next few months instead. After finishing all the courses up to PADI dive master and leading out diving groups for that season, I became bored with paradise, beginning to run out of reasons to stay.

I soon found another challenge; completing a commercial diving ticket because it seemed like fun, even toying with the idea of staying in this industry if there was money to be made. After two months in Durban's Professional Diving Institute, I had new qualifications in the wallet, but little use for them. Without additional specialties such as underwater welding or non-destructive testing, there weren't many worthwhile opportunities. There was diamond diving off the west coast, but I'd heard of too many horror stories; there was ship salvage work available, but it didn't pay very well. I didn't want to work on an oil rig either. And, oh yes, I had to get back to reality.

After close to a year of sun tanning and living in shorts, I was broke. It forced me to do something I hadn't in eight years; I approached David's brother, Abel Mapena, for a temporary job. After '92, I thought I'd seen the last of trucking, but life has strange twists and turns.

Abel agreed to give me work for about two months, paying per trip, or until I had enough to buy a plane ticket. My friends in England had offered to sponsor my stay when I arrived. Truckers who'd survived the Mozambique run, those still doing this same route, were glad to see me.

Joe was pulling Zambia only, Jimmy mostly Angola, others Malawi. Few would ever leave this industry; it has something to do with 'when diesel gets in your veins'. Whether by choice or accident, this fraternity had become somewhat of a distant family. What this return also revealed was that things I'd largely forgotten, had a deeper emotional significance than I'd been aware of.

Abel's work was primarily thirty ton loads of sugar from Durban to Maputo with an ERF truck he had just repaired. Coincidentally this was via Swaziland and the Namaacha border post, like before. The route from Johannesburg to Maputo through Ressano Garcia was highway with a toll gate now—part of the new-look Mozambique in a rebuilding phase.

Namaacha border control, October 2000

"Joe Cocker, Bob Marley, Otis Redding…"

"What else you got?" I asked the music pirate.

"*Musica Brasileira, musica da terra.*" He flipped through the cassettes stacked like dominoes on the dirty wooden box. Compact disks, or CDs, hadn't taken off in Mozambique just yet.

"No *Djumba djumba? Quanto cada?*" How much each?

"Ten thou," he stated using two hands and fingers as I turned away from the glare bouncing off the cassette's covers.

"*Dá la o Joe Cocker.*" I picked one up. It had a cheap looking copy of the original masquerading as a cover, an off-centered label on the cassette said 'Side A' and 'Side B'. "Are you sure Joe Cocker sings on this?" I queried in English.

"*Sim, Sim*, very good. *Muito soul.*"

"Can I test it first?" I negotiated, dreading that I would find some horrible rap music instead. Not for the first time, either.

"You've got *apparelation*?" He asked in anglo-fied Portuguese.

"What's that?"

"*Aparelhagem.*" Sound system. He clarified.

"It's Ok. Here's the money."

Forcing my way through the queues, and stench of unwashed bodies, I walked into the darkened offices of immigration. That distinct, sharp smell was still here.

"It is your first time in Mozambique?" The dark man asked me, perusing through a brand-new passport.

"First time since the war, yes." He looked at me quizzically, as if there had never been a war. I strolled out of the building, shunning the bright sun as I dropped the sunglasses over my eyes.

The past was awakened as soon as I drove out of the border post; it felt like yesterday I'd been here. As I exited the boom towards Maputo, the road pulled right on an uphill, past an informal market of wooden stalls.

During the war a South African trucker with an unforgettable yellow Oshkosh truck slept overnight on this hill's crest. In the morning, it wouldn't start so he unhitched it from his trailer. As any driver knows, unless the engine runs, the compressor cannot build enough air pressure to release the brakes, it's immovable. What happened next is open to speculation; this is what we believe he did. After loosening the brakes with a fourteen spanner on the slack adjusters, he found help from pedestrians passing by to push the truck into a rolling start downhill. The clutch wouldn't have worked without air pressure, and he wouldn't have been able to get the truck into gear. He must've forgotten that.

H, who was parked at the entrance of the border gate, heard the commotion that ensued, sounds of crunching vehicles followed by a lot of gunfire. The Oshkosh and its now dead driver came to a halt a dozen meters away. H jumped out from his rig, asking a soldier still pointing his rifle at the back of the tractor what was going on. And what did he shoot the South African driver for? His reply was that the truck had just killed a soldier as well as two civilians as it crashed into a row of parked minibuses.

Driving under a long row of eucalyptus trees, the military checkpoint two or so kilometers past the town, no longer existed. Even when it had, it didn't always help much. An attack on one of Braam's trucks was less than a kilometer from the boom, within sight of the military. The barefoot bandits—his driver's words—ordered the truck fifty meters away from the road and set it on fire there. The driver was let go. It was said that attacks on this corridor started right from the very entrance into it. This wasn't an exaggeration; one truck was attacked less than three hundred meters from the checkpoint.

A few surprises and ironies awaited en route to Maputo.

Now, it was a brand new, tarred road which didn't fit the frame of memory. It didn't follow the exact same path as before; some areas were unrecognizable. I wanted to take a lumbering drive towards the capital to absorb the memories, but before I realized, I was almost in Boane. Whereas it would have taken two hours in those days, it now took less than a third of the time. Cars screamed around the bends and blew past me; there was nothing of that old, slow, treacherous road.

Where soldiers once stood and vehicles were ablaze, was a now a huge billboard on the side of the road, an advertisement cum notice board reminding people to wear condoms. This was normal for a country decimated by the AIDS epidemic, but the content was a little cynical. On the forefront of the picture was an African woman handing a man a bright condom, in the background was a line of trucks. My first impression was the not-so-subtle characterization of truckers.

This billboard was placed in the vicinity where Joseph was hit, where his truck was shot up. He survived that attack, but died in 1995 from AIDS. He drove buses until the end, when he was just skin and bone on a gaunt face. He'd also been rammed by a military vehicle near here.

"It was that V-shaped, troop carrier thing," David described it. It must have been a Russian BTR, a FAM mine proof vehicle. Equally puzzling is when they hauled him out of the truck, and beat him to a pulp with rifle butts. Another South African trucker whose overall-wearing assistant had army boots on was accused of being a '*soldado*'; he too was beaten up. This road had a few mysteries to unravel.

Not having much joy with drivers, Harry closed down his operation. Gary, the other white driver on the Mozambique run drove into a packed restaurant in downtown Maputo one evening. He'd just picked up some ladies after having too much to drink. By the time he left, he had written off two trucks. Then there was Timothy's death which Harry didn't take too well; he loved his drivers. Perhaps the reason he didn't close shop sooner was the Mozambican gift of understatement having rubbed off on Timothy. It's not true of course, but I'd like to think that he didn't realize how deadly the roads were. Especially with Timothy's calm, relaxed tone when explaining the *situação*.

It was shocking to discover how many drivers had become HIV positive; equally alarming was the extent of my naivety. I wasn't the only one. The virus devastated 1990s South Africa, growing worse into the 2000s when the government was in denial about the problem. Our Ministry of Health remained hesitant about treating people living with HIV. Although there were cheap ARVs in the global market, the South African government refused to make it available until 2003.

A few hundred meters past the first billboard stood a more eye-catching one, an advertisement for a local beer. There was a picture of a man and woman dancing close in a sensual way, promoting casual sex. This tag line was 'passion without limits'. The woman in the condom ad was dressed like a schoolteacher whereas this one was dressed like a prostitute. That irony wasn't lost on me; even so, trucking was still a major culprit of spreading AIDS in Africa. A third of the drivers from the Mozambique run would die of HIV-related deaths. Another third died from attacks and accidents on the corridors; only the remainder were still alive at the turn of the millennium. Those are worse statistics than active armies in war.

Near the old military checkpoint at Boane was a broken-down bus on the fork to Moamba; it reminded me of something droll. A friend had once come upon an accident here—a horrific collision between a bus and a truck. The fire brigade was busy cutting up the mangled passenger vehicle to retrieve the bodies when he warned the fireman cutting into the bus' skin with a jaws of life. Just then the rescue worker cut off a man's hand along with a piece of sheet metal.

"Doesn't matter, he's already dead," he quipped and threw the hand into the bush. It was on this same spot that FAM was stopping every car to help transport a pile of injured to hospital after an attack in 1984. "There were so many bodies that blood was dripping from doors of loaded cars. Women were ripping up their *capulanas* to use as tourniquets, and bodies were being stuffed on top of each other," Vera told me. The Mozambican government had never been equipped to deal with mass casualties.

The corridors had mystical qualities; people often spoke of having a premonition. Vera was supposed to travel with Joe and H on that fateful trip, but was sent home instead, H had a 'bad feeling' about it. There are many stories of foreboding with a palpable heaviness being felt before attacks happened. In this atmosphere of heightened senses, there was also an instinct about people. Braam once came into Mozambique with a *bakkie*, a pickup truck on some business. He used the Ressano road before it closed, and although bearable for light vehicles, it was never a good idea.

Just past the border he gave two soldiers a ride. Instead of allowing him to continue on the main road towards Moamba, they directed him onto a small side road. He had a gnawing sense they were taking him to a remote spot for execution, to loot his belongings. After stalling them by offering food and money, which they accepted, he still had a horrible suspicion he was about to die. It had been pouring and the roads were slippery, when they came across a mud patch that looked impossible to cross, he barely succeeded in reversing out. Turning back, he sped up towards the main road from where they'd veered off. His passengers said nothing until he dropped them off.

Driving through the new look Boane town, something was missing; where there'd once been playful, cheering kids was now a fuel garage, and new businesses growing alongside it. Briefly, I missed being welcomed by those laughs and chortles, those beaming smiles. They were probably better off today.

The consequences of my last trip were at the forefront of my mind, causing some apprehension. I had to offload at the Manica warehouse where I'd once been banned. Butterflies danced around my stomach, but I'd been told it was no longer an issue.

Nearing Matola, I pushed the cassette I'd just bought into the tape deck; it turned out to be a decent album. The words in one particular number, '*standing knee deep in a river (dying of thirst)*' grabbed me. It was a song Don Williams had written, the one on the cassette Timothy had given me in '91. The gist of it was having taken friendships for granted. Not every word was relatable, but Joe Cocker's delivery of the song with his gritty voice was simply engrossing. I tried to slow to a leisurely speed, trying to breathe in the moment, but couldn't focus. Cars were zipping past and I had to concentrate on impatient and moronic drivers. The traffic had really grown here, annoyingly so.

The most ironic aspect of the Mozambique run was the dramatic rise in road deaths after the war. As roads and infrastructure were repaired traffic volume increased when the well-to-do of Maputo headed for the towns and beaches up north. Speeding and inexperience caused most fatalities. Maputo's drivers were not used to highways; on the stretch between Ressano Garcia and Nelspruit, on the South African side, the amount of accidents caused by Mozambicans was staggering. This trend had changed little over the last few years; H once remarked that 'they were dying like flies' on these roads. They weren't dying at this rate during the war when the intent to kill and maim was an actual, official objective.

Maputo was now a city being modernized. A $1.3-billion aluminum smelter was being built on its outskirts, and foreign investment was pouring in. There was a lot of activity, especially in construction being seen everywhere; new restaurants and busy sidewalk cafes had cropped up. There were showrooms with luxury cars and SUVs, and the supermarkets had full shelves.

Food supply had come a long way, I remember a cousin who'd lived in Mozambique visiting us in South Africa in 1987. When we took her to a supermarket, she had to walk out after seeing so much food because she felt 'light-headed and disorientated'. But with full bellies emerged new problems; along with privatization and economic reforms came new forms of economic gangsterism, and crony capitalism. There were banking scandals and deaths of those exposing them, new and more sophisticated crimes were being committed.

These new sagas were also exposing an ineffective justice system. With the growing market economy also came kidnappings of the wealthy and hijackings of expensive vehicles. Mozambique's economic growth was nearly 8% yearly on average, but it hadn't profited the general population or significantly reduced poverty. Notably for me, trucks were forbidden inside the town, but street kids still begged there with many new luxury cars to harass now.

An unconditional general amnesty for the years 1976-1992 was passed in Parliament. Neither Frelimo, nor Renamo's mass crimes would be punished and victims would never see justice. Years later, Soloman Mondlane challenged Frelimo to create a Truth and Reconciliation Commission (TRC).

Graça Machel, Samora's wife who seemed obsessed with finding those responsible for her husband's death in an air crash in October 1986, was also challenged. Mondlane asked why she was separating this from the rest of the issues that took place under Samora's regime. "It is unfair. We also want to know what happened to our relatives and something must be done to compensate the victims [of Machel's regime]," He said. (Charles Phahlane, "*Mozambican activists want their own TRC*" www.iol.co.za, 3rd June 2003)

The cause of Machel's death is an unsettled topic with no shortage of suspects and opinions. The apartheid regime's hand in the 'assassination', and high-ranking Frelimo leaders make up the top two. On the 19th of October 1986, a Soviet Tupolev 134 jet returning from a summit in Zambia flew into the Mbuzini Mountains in Mpumalanga, South Africa. Thirty-three of the forty-four people on board were killed, including the president.

Drunken Russian pilots, the weather, being lured off course by a false radio beacon transmitting on the same frequency as Maputo airport, or the one that Swaziland had just erected, are all disputed theories. The cockpit voice recorder reveals that the flight crew believed they were making their final approach at 21:21 PM, and still querying Maputo about the unlit runway.

Renamo were operating out of bases in Malawi which had drawn the ire of Machel. At a news conference a few weeks previously, he had threatened to place missiles along the Malawi border, and to close off traffic to South African transport transiting Mozambique. Shortly thereafter, a landmine exploded near the Mozambique border, injuring SADF troops. South Africa may have had reasons to eliminate him, but so did elements within Frelimo; Machel wanted to get rid of ministers who were profiting from the war. Among the odd things that happened the evening of the crash was a power failure, a total blackout in Maputo. At 22:00, as the lights came back on, Marcelino Dos Santos, Machel's deputy, delivered the news to the nation on television and radio.

Some Mozambicans contend that the President had lost support, and was operating on his decisions alone. Another notable event was the recent change of aircraft that his delegation normally travelled in. Often overlooked is also Machel's visit to the US and his meeting with Reagan in September 1985, which wouldn't have pleased Moscow. By now he had trodden on a few toes, including God's.

A month before Machel died, he challenged God, or tried to eliminate him—only he knows what. With thousands of witnesses to this drama an animated Samora told a stunned rally in Machava, as well as those listening on radio, that God didn't exist and he would prove it. He cursed and blasphemed, then gave God sixty seconds to strike him dead for it. Pulling out a stopwatch in front of a mesmerized crowd he clicked it. Tick-tick… until the minute was up. '*Aonde está Deus?*' Where is God?

In the wreckage, a document was found outlining Zimbabwe and Mozambique's imminent plot to overthrow the conservative government of Malawi. Such an event could have widened the conflict with a regional war, forcing South Africa to defend their ally, Malawi.

To my surprise, Renamo came close to winning the national election in 1999. Frelimo's Joaquim Chissano was re-elected with 52.3% of the votes, against 47.7% for the leader of Renamo, Afonso Dhlakama. They rejected the official results, alleging widespread electoral fraud, a claim rejected by the Supreme Court.

A cousin of mine who had moved from Portugal to Mozambique in the mid-1990s, joined Renamo. During our chat, he was adamant that Frelimo had stolen the elections, explaining the shenanigans in detail, something echoed by other Mozambican folk. To me, the general results only proved that half the population did not think Renamo was the devil, but it also showed that the other half did. Some of the ex-rebel leaders were now living in Maputo; Daniel even did a furniture load for Dhlakama's residence. I asked if he'd confronted the man about the fact that it was probably his men that had shot him. He simply replied, "No."

Earlier that year, in February and March, five weeks of heavy rainfall brought flooding across southern Mozambique. The Incomati, the Umbeluzi, and the Limpopo rivers burst their banks, and even engulfed portions of Maputo. David described a picture of hundreds of Coca-Cola crates drifting all along the Matola to Maputo highway. The floods caused widespread devastation, bringing disease and displacing close to half a million people. It was considered to be the country's worst natural disaster.

These events aired on international television; one woman even gave birth on a tree as stranded peasants waited for choppers to airlift them. But any tragedy in Mozambique would not be complete without corruption. Donor food, including truckloads of protein biscuits, were being sold to village elders in hardest hit areas for cattle or currency, one trucker told me. If these rains had been a type of cleansing for the stained earth, they needed much more of it.

H was still pulling loads for Manica. I joined him at the new premises in Machava where we would both offload. As we walked towards his truck, he stopped and remarked, "Hey, do you remember this guy?" He pointed to a middle-aged man standing at the entrance to the warehouse.

"No, is he a driver?"

"That's the guy you had a fight with. I still laugh when I think about it. Apparently, he can be a quite *hardegat* on his day." The supervisor saw us and must have recognized me, because he had a cautious smile. I walked up to him and we shook hands.

"*Então, vamos beber uma cerjeva?*" So, are we going to have a beer? He asked. I understood it as I should buy him a beer, but H corrected me later. Handing him some money, he smiled and walked away. It was all forgotten.

"Hey, H, play us a song," I said, sitting back on the passenger seat of his truck.

"Well, you know, a man once said money and riches may not change you, but time will take you on," a cheerful H said.

"Yah, play a song, don't quote one," I joked.

He picked up the old, banged up acoustic guitar from his bunk. He strummed with his one good foot tapping on the truck floor, moving his head backwards and forward, his upper body swaying to the rhythm as he grooved to the song. He closed his eyes, as he picked the strings and sang with his unique, raspy voice.

'I don't want to be the one who says I'm sorry…I don't want to be the one who takes the blame. All the bad times should be forgotten, all the sad times should be erased. Does not make a difference, where you think you're going…just please remember not to slam the door…'

At times, he seemed to forget the words to a song, and just made something up instead. It could give a whole new meaning to it. In the Rodriguez's 'Rich Folks Hoax' he would use 'I never could congest' instead of 'digest'; I kept correcting him but he kept singing his version.

"How is the computer world out there?" He asked, winding down the strumming.

"It can be fulfilling, but it's also a rat race with its share of ambitious, greedy people."

"Ag, it's like that anywhere."

"I miss the simplicity here, of trucking."

"Hey, broer, it's not always that simple. I've been in Africa a long time. I've been locked up and shot at more times than you can imagine. They've accused me of being everything from a saboteur to a spy. Me, a truck driver…" He laughed heartedly "Once, in Zambia, I was locked up for something as ridiculous as that, I don't remember what it was. Anyway, I asked to take my guitar into the cell with me. Sitting alone there, I played some *lekker* Chuck Berry songs, and really hit the groove you know. Next minute, I had some of the police around me in the cell. They fetched some of the beers in my truck, and we had ourselves a good party. I was wearing a policeman's cap at one stage. I even had one of them playing my guitar. The next morning, they let me go saying politely thank you, Mister H."

H had missed the point I was trying to make, instead making a smooth transition into his own adventures.

"You seem to have more lives than even Tim had." I added.

"Ja, *broer*, it's sad, man. All the good guys seem to get taken out," H went on "But Timothy made his choices and stuck by them. Now, I'll tell you a story. That night after Tim's death, a lot of us that went to the accident site stopped over at a restaurant on the way back. You know, one of these restaurants in a small town (Maxixe) that never receives any customers. We sat around; some guys were really sad; anyway, we ordered prawns. Now, the prawns took forever to come, I think they had to fish for the bloody things. David took out some stash, enough for a joint. I think it was out of Tim's wallet. So, we all smoked a joint in Timothy's memory. I tell you, that high on that night I will never forget. I can't explain it to you. Now, Mauro, he is way goofed on the joint, and even drunker on the cheap white wine this restaurant conjured up. So, the prawns arrive and Mauro pours *peri-peri* [chili] sauce all over the prawns like it was tomato sauce. You know… the guys are hungry. I'm famished, so we gulped down the prawns like it was snacks. Man, I tell you, that stuff burned like s★★t! Wow! Whenever I think of it, it burns."

H's account of this event had no deeper meaning, but there may have been a metaphor in there somewhere. It was just his thoughts cushioned with a brand of humor I'd gotten accustomed to from him. I couldn't fault him; he was the one with the lively mind, the one that saw the lighter side of things.

"How's trucking nowadays?" I asked.

"*Ag,* still a grind. Every time I sit down in a pub in say, Buffalo, some bloke comes and parks next to me to ask about my missing leg. I explain, and for the next hour he slobbers all over you. At the end of the night, he is drunk out of his mind, never mind fascinated, and still hasn't understood a bloody thing. It's a bar story, nothing more. The idiot probably envies my leg and thinks it's cool, too! What he doesn't understand is that I fight a daily battle to keep this truck running."

"I didn't hear you complain when all the ladies come ask you to dance, to see you spin on that peg leg."

"Well, *broer.* It has its advantages!" H laughed with a sly look. "Women love a mysterious man." Stories from the war had ended in '*incrível pá!*' Other than that, nothing much had changed.

Our banter petered off as silence came between us. I watched a palm tree calmly swaying gently in the wind, ruminating on the emotional pull this place once had. H and Vera weren't together any longer; I hadn't seen my girl in years, but the past wasn't only about that. When Bob Dylan wrote a breezy song about Mozambique in 1975, he said it was magic in a magical land—the sunny sky is aqua blue, lots of pretty girls, and lovely people living free. The fading images of bell bottoms, 70s long hair, big afros, Coca-Cola, and happy people in a tropical paradise were still here, even if only in memory.

The Mozambique run had been more than a romantic tale of beautiful deserted beaches, exotic women, and death roads. It was about the inexplicable lure, the rush, a buzz around the whole experience. Moreover, it was about the small community I'd come to know, the incredible friendships I'd forged, and a trucking spirit I cannot describe. It was about the strangers we'd encountered along the way, and expressions etched on people's faces. They were unforgettable.

Mozambique's misery, so candidly portrayed in their art, in that gallery where I'd met her, had abated. The mood had changed; trucking here felt like a hamster wheel, like gears in a growing capitalist machine, a cynic might say. Although hunger dominated Mozambique during the war, I'd always felt a tangible energy, a spirited optimism, a vibrancy. People were polite, helpful and tolerant in those days; this was less evident now. Back then everybody was going through the same predicament, which created a sense of brotherhood. That vibe had evaporated with the mists of time.

What really matters is that the hell run was my valley of the shadow of death; I learnt how to pray here. Goodness and mercy followed me on this arduous road. In October 1992, the weekend after my last trip, I made peace with God through my Lord, and Savior Jesus Christ. I never went back to my old ways; what emerged from Mozambique's hell run was a new man.

★　★　★

Thank you for reading this book. For more stories and photos visit the blog at www.miguelmitras.com

South African slang and phrases in this book

Ag – The Afrikaans equivalent to 'oh'. A guttural pronunciation from the Dutch 'ach'.

Bedonnerd – Out of temper, crazy.

Brekers – Scrappers.

Broer – Afrikaans for brother. Also used is 'bru', a term of affection in close friendships. **Bra** is the equivalent from people of Cape descent.

Boer – Literally 'farmer', sometimes used as a derogatory term for white South Afrikaans.

Eish – Used to express a range of emotions, such as surprise, annoyance, or resignation.

Fokof – Go away. Goes fast.

Hardegat – Hard assed.

Hoesit – How's it? As in 'how are you doing?'

Ja – Literally 'yes', the 'j' is pronounced like the 'y' in 'yes'. '**Ja swaer**' is an affirmation.

Jong – Emphasis.

Kwaai – Cool or great, can also be used for 'angry'.

Lekker – Good, great.

Mag – Force.

Moer – Give a hiding.

Mos – Implies that what has been said is well known or self-evident. The closest English equivalent would be 'duh!'

Porras – Slang for Portuguese, not necessarily derogatory.

Pasop – Watch out.

Skyf – A Joint.

Skrik – Fright.

Smokkled – Toyed with. Also means smuggle.

Ouens – Guys.

Toppie – Old man, in an endearing sort of way.

You mos make out? – Are you picturing it?

Yah – 'Yes' or 'yeah'. The same as 'Ja' without the Afrikaans accent.